ROCK 'N' ROLL TRIVIA

Cover photos:
Elliott Landy/Images; Laura Levine; Linda Matlow/Pix Int'l.;
Michael Ochs Archives; Paul Natkin/Photo Reserve; Rex
Features/RDR Productions; Scope Features/RDR Productions;
Ron Wolfson/Mega; Joe Bangay/Pix Int'l.
Photo credits:
Brian Aris/RDR Productions: p. 54; Randy Bachman/Pix. Int'l.:
p. 19; Joe Bangay/Pix Int'l.: p. 30; Images: pp. 43, 48; Gene
Kirkland/Pix Int'l.: p.46; Kriegsmann/Michael Ochs Archives:
p. 47, Elliott Landy/Images, p.22; Laura Levine: pp. 11, 14,
19, 27, 36, 40, 53. 56; David Magnus/RDR Productions: p. 55;
Ross Marino: p. 44; Linda Matlow/Pix Int'l.: p. 52; Paul
Natkin/Photo Reserve: pp. 2, 5, 9, 13, 15, 20, 26, 29, 32, 33,
34, 40, 45, 48, 49, 51, 53, 54, 64; Michael Ochs Archives:
pp. 2, 4, 5, 6, 7, 8, 9, 10, 13, 15, 16, 18, 21, 23, 25, 26, 28,
31, 32, 34, 35, 38, 41, 46, 50, 54, 56, 57; Laurie Paladino/Pix
Int'l.: p. 14; Robin Platzer/Images: p. 50; Rex Features/RDR
Productions: pp. 3, 6, 12, 17, 27, 29, 36,42; Mick Rock/Images:
p. 41; John Schwartz/Images: p. 38; Scope/RDR Productions:
p. 44; Bob Sorce/Pix Int'l.: p. 48; David Sygall: pp. 16, 23,
28; Allen Tannenbaum/Images: pp. 42, 43; Mark Weiss/Rogers
and Cowan: p. 61.

Copyright © 1985 by Publications International, Ltd.
All rights reserved.
This book may not be reproduced or quoted in whole or in
part by mimeograph or any other printed means or for
presentation on radio, television, videotape, or film without
written permission from:

Louis Weber, President
Publications International, Ltd.
3841 West Oakton Street
Skokie, Illinois 60076

*ML
3534
@64
1985*

Writers: Noë Goldwasser and Bill Dahl

Permission is never granted for commercial purposes.

Manufactured in the United States of America
10 9 8 7 6 5 4 3 2 1

ISBN: 0-517-47933-8

This edition published by:
Beekman House
Distributed by Crown Publishers, Inc.
One Park Avenue
New York, New York 10016

CONTENTS

THE ALLMAN BROTHERS

7. Both Duane Allman and Berry Oakley died in motorcycle accidents within a year of each other. What else was coincidental about their deaths?

8. When Gregg's personal manager was busted for drugs, Gregg testified against him. What is his name?

9. What band did Dickey Betts form in 1977?

10. Gregg Allman and Cher released what album together?

11. Who is Elijah Blue?

12. Which Allman Brothers Band members went on to form the group Sea Level?

13. Duane Allman played on a 1971 debut album that was produced by *Rolling Stone* publisher Jann Wenner. Whose debut was it?

14. Where does the album title *Eat A Peach* come from?

15. What Jackson Browne song did Gregg Allman record on his first solo LP?

1. Which of these bands did Gregg and Duane head before forming The Allman Brothers Band?
A. The Kings; **B.** The Allman Joys; **C.** Hourglass; **D.** The 31st Of February.

2. Duane Allman was the primary session guitarist at what studio?

3. Who produced The Allman Joys' first single?

4. Duane Allman did session work with all except one of the following. Which one?
A. Aretha Franklin; **B.** Clarence Carter; **C.** Stevie Wonder; **D.** Percy Sledge; **E.** King Curtis.

5. Duane Allman worked with Eric Clapton to record what classic rock single?

6. Where and when did The Allman Brothers Band record its first live album?

The Allman Brothers (left to right): Butch Trucks, Dickey Betts, Berry Oakley, Duane Allman, Gregg Allman, Jai Johnny Johanson.   Dickey Betts (inset).

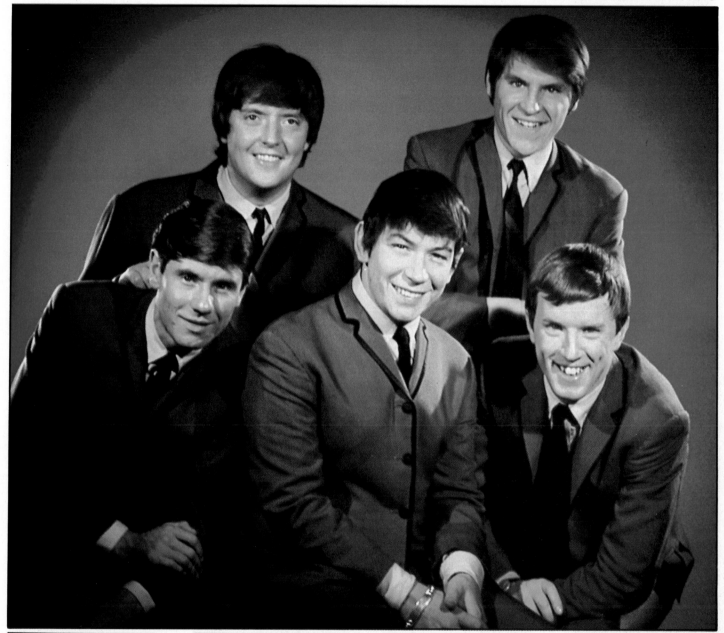

1. The Animals sang "We Gotta Get Out Of This Place." What place did they have to get out of?

2. What was The Animals' only #1 U.S. hit?

3. "The House Of The Rising Sun" introduced a new instrument to rock 'n' roll. What was it?

4. The Animals recorded an ode to a rock festival. Name it.

5. Which Animal went on to found and record with War?

6. Which Animal wrote the sound track for and appeared in the film *O Lucky Man?*

7. Where did The Animals get their name?

8. The Animals were in a film about co-eds. Name it.

9. List these bands from earliest to latest:
A. The Alan Price Combo;
B. Eric Burdon And The Animals; **C.** The New Animals; **D.** The Animals.

10. A member of the original Animals went on to manage Jimi Hendrix and then Slade. What is his name?

11. What rock guitarist of the late '70s and '80s was a member of The New Animals for a short time in 1968?

12. Why did Alan Price leave The Animals?

13. In 1981, Burdon starred in and composed the sound track for what film?

14. In 1976–1977, the original Animals reunited for an album. Name it.

The Animals (left to right, top): Chas Chandler, Alan Price; (bottom): Hilton Valentine, Eric Burdon, John Steel.

THE BAND

1. Who is the only American member of The Band?

2. Who brought the group to New York to perform and record in 1964?

3. Which members of The Band backed Bob Dylan on his debut electric Forest Hills concert of August 28, 1965?

4. The Band's first album was titled *Music From Big Pink*. What was "Big Pink"?

5. What prominent Irish musician appeared on the *Cahoots* album?

6. Which of The Band's albums was a tribute to early rock 'n' roll?

7. Robbie Robertson went on to produce Neil Diamond's first platinum album. Name the album.

8. The Band—minus one member—toured with Dylan until his 1966 motorcycle accident. Then, that member rejoined The Band. Who was the reinstated member?

9. After Dylan went into seclusion following his 1966 motorcycle accident, he recorded an album with The Band. The album was released in 1975. Name it.

10. The film featuring The Band's final concert is considered one of the finest rock 'n' roll movies ever made. Name the film and the director.

11. What band did Levon Helm form after The Band broke up?

12. In what film did Helm make his acting debut?

13. What 1980 film release did Robbie Robertson score, co-star in, and produce?

14. Where did Robertson make his debut solo vocal appearance?

The Band (left to right): Levon Helm, Garth Hudson, Robbie Robertson, Rick Danko, Richard Manuel (inset).

1. Since The Beach Boys began recording in 1961, how many of their singles have gone gold?

2. In real life, who was the "Surfer Girl"?

3. Who was the only Beach Boy who actually surfed?

4. Who of the following were *not* members of The Beach Boys?
A. Carl Wilson; **B.** Murray Wilson; **C.** Brian Wilson; **D.** Al Jardine.

5. Which of The Beach Boys was partially deaf?

6. In what year did Capitol Records release *Beach Boys '69?* (Hint: It wasn't 1969.)

7. On 1978's *M.I.U. Album,* what do the initials stand for?

8. What former country superstar played lead guitar on "Good Vibrations"?

9. What was the name of the record label owned by The Beach Boys? What other artist released an album on that label?

10. How many different U.S. labels did The Beach Boys record on?

11. Mike Love collaborated with what jazz flautist and fellow T.M. follower on the album *Celebration?*

12. Which Beach Boys album contained only instrumental tracks?

13. What Beach Boys song did Bryan Ferry and Keith Moon both cover?

14. Which member of The Beach Boys was friendly with Charles Manson, and what song did Manson claim to have co-written?

15. True or False: New York City's Joffrey Ballet company once performed a ballet set entirely to Beach Boys music.

The Beach Boys (left to right): Brian Wilson, Mike Love, Carl Wilson, David Marks, Dennis Wilson.

Brian Wilson of The Beach Boys (inset).

THE BEATLES

1. Which of these classic Beatles hits did *not* make the U.S. Top 40?
A. "She Loves You"; **B.** "All My Loving"; **C.** "I Saw Her Standing There"; **D.** "Can't Buy Me Love."

2. What was The Beatles' very first U.S. Top 40 hit?

3. What was The Beatles' first single of any kind?

4. Before Ringo, there was Pete Best. But who was the drummer before him?

5. Who was the first Beatle to leave the group, and what instrument did he play?

6. What did Beatles manager Brian Epstein do for a living before he met the Fab Four?

7. What critical events took place on June 6 and August 17 of 1962?

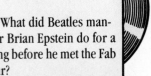

8. Match the song title with the real-life inspiration: 1. "Hey Jude"; 2. "Martha My Dear"; 3. "Julia"; 4. "Sexy Sadie"
A. a dog; **B.** John's mother; **C.** Maharishi Mahesh Yogi; **D.** a Beatle's child.

9. According to *Billboard* magazine's charts, how many Beatles albums were ranked as the top album of the year?

10. What 1965 hit was originally titled "Scrambled Egg"?

11. Where and when did The Beatles' last scheduled public performance take place?

12. What do the following performers have in common: The Beatles, Billy Preston, Ronnie Spector, James Taylor, and The Modern Jazz Quartet?

13. What do *these* performers have in common: Billy J. Kramer And The Dakotas, Tommy Quickly, Peter And Gordon, Mary Hopkin, and Cilla Black?

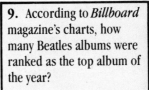

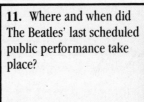

The Beatles discover psychedelia: Paul McCartney, George Harrison, Ringo Starr, John Lennon.

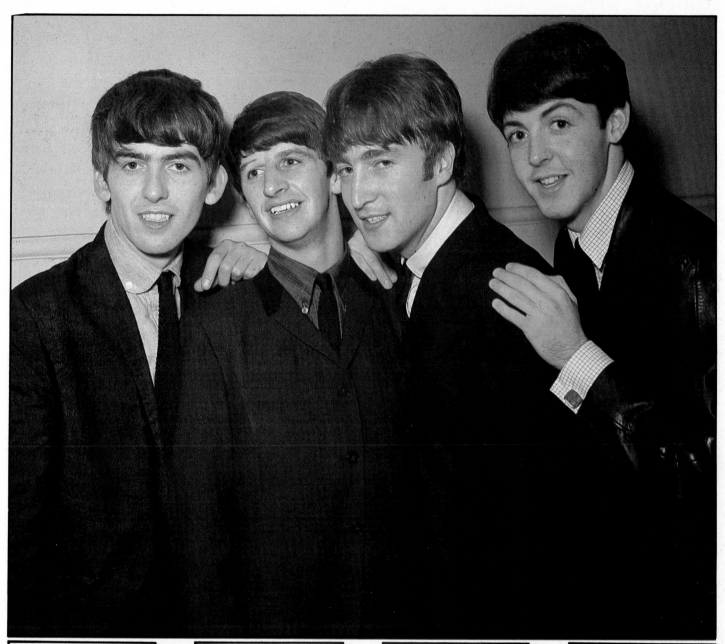

14. What guitar legend married George's first wife, Patti?

15. What Beatles album was available only in America, and what was so unusual about its cover?

16. Which of the following is *not* an actual place in Britain?
A. Penny Lane; **B.** Strawberry Fields; **C.** Blue Jay Way; **D.** Abbey Road.

17. How did quizzical Joan, who was "studying metaphysical science," meet her end?

18. What was so unusual about "Maggie Mae," a short song on *Let It Be?*

19. In the "funeral procession" on the back cover of *Abbey Road,* who was dressed as the preacher? The grave digger? The mourner?

20. According to the "Paul Is Dead" theory, who replaced Paul in the band?

21. In "Strawberry Fields," John apparently says "I buried Paul." What did John insist he said?

22. What group once covered an entire Beatles album, song for song?

23. What Beatles song has been recorded by more artists (about 1,200) than any other?

24. What song was originally titled "Ringo's Theme" when it was used as background music on the sound track to *A Hard Day's Night?*

25. The Beatles had several earlier names. Which *wasn't* one of them?
A. The Quarrymen; **B.** Johnny And The Moondogs; **C.** The Silver Beatles; **D.** Rory Storme And The Hurricanes.

The Beatles (left to right): George Harrison, Ringo Starr, John Lennon, Paul McCartney.

THE BEE GEES

1. Of three Bee Gees, which are the twins?

2. What does the band's name signify?

3. Where did the trio achieve their early fame?

4. What current record company magnate became their manager in 1967?

5. What syndicated TV show did younger brother Andy once host?

6. What was the first Bee Gees song to hit the American record charts?
A. "Spicks And Specks"; **B.** "Three Kisses Of Love"; **C.** "New York Mining Disaster 1941"; **D.** "How Can You Mend A Broken Heart."

7. On what show did the band make their American TV debut?

8. Which of the brothers produced and sang with Barbra Streisand on her 1980 album *Guilty?*

9. True or False: *Saturday Night Fever* was the first movie soundtrack to top *Billboard* magazine's year-end album charts.

10. For how long did *Saturday Night Fever* hold the record for worldwide album sales?

11. Who was "How Deep Is Your Love" originally written for?

12. In March, 1978, five of the Top 10 songs on the charts were either co-written or co-produced by The Bee Gees. How many of these did they record themselves?

13. Which of the following artists did *not* hit with a song written and produced by a member of The Bee Gees?
A. Yvonne Elliman; **B.** Neil Sedaka; **C.** Frankie Valli; **D.** Dionne Warwick.

14. What English pop singer married Maurice?

15. Several years ago, the Bee Gees were taken to court and accused of stealing the music for one of their number one hits. Which one?

The Bee Gees (left to right): Robin Gibb, Maurice Gibb, Barry Gibb, Colin Peterson.

1. Name one of Chuck Berry's occupations prior to playing rock 'n' roll.

2. What is the name of Berry's patented rock 'n' roll stroll?

3. What is the name of Berry's first single?

4. What is the name of Berry's *only* number one pop single?

5. Which one of these 1950s films did Berry *not* appear in:
A. *Rock, Rock, Rock;* **B.** *Rock Around The Clock;* **C.** *Mr. Rock And Roll;* **D.** *Go, Johnny, Go!*

6. Name two sequels to "Johnny B. Goode."

7. What car did Berry's Ford beat in "Maybellene"?

8. What is Berry Park?

9. What was the original name of "Maybellene," and where did the new name come from?

10. In what film did Chuck Berry and Bo Diddley jam together?

11. What Chicago blues great first steered Berry to Chess Records?
A. Willie Dixon; **B.** Johnnie Johnson; **C.** Muddy Waters; **D.** Bo Diddley.

12. For what offense was Berry arrested in 1959?

13. Berry wrote the first song that The Rolling Stones ever recorded. Name it.

14. Why did Berry reportedly assault Stones guitarist Keith Richards?

15. In 1979, Berry pulled 100 days in prison for what offense?

Chuck Berry

Chuck Berry poses with his favorite house plant.

DAVID BOWIE

8. Which of the following are real people?
A. Iggy Pop; **B.** Screamin' Lord Byron; **C.** Ziggy Stardust; **D.** Zowie Bowie.

9. What color are Bowie's eyes?

10. Name the 1969 song about Major Tom and its 1979 sequel. Name the albums they appear on.

11. What is the title of Bowie's first collection of greatest hits?

12. What Rolling Stones song was purportedly about Bowie's wife?

1. What is David Bowie's real name, and why did he have to change it just as he was beginning to get noticed?

2. Bowie's art teacher (and the headmaster of Bromley Technical School) was the father of what well-known guitar star?

3. Which of the following careers has Bowie *not* entered professionally: **A.** commercial artist; **B.** mime; **C.** clothing designer; **D.** backing musician.

4. Who is Major Tom and how did he die?

5. The co-composer of Bowie's first number one single also sang harmony on the record. Name the song and the singer.

6. Which of the following will Bowie confirm about himself?
A. Bowie is gay; **B.** Bowie is straight; **C.** Bowie is bisexual; **D.** all of the above.

7. Which of the following films does *not* feature Bowie?
A. *Merry Christmas, Mr. Lawrence;* **B.** *The Hunger;* **C.** *Cat People;* **D.** *The Man Who Fell To Earth.*

13. Who (or what) were The Spiders From Mars?

14. True or False: Bowie starred in a stage production of *The Elephant Man* on Broadway.

15. What do the following groups have in common? The King Bees; The Manish Boys; and David Jones And The Lower Third.

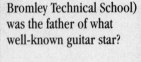

A young David Bowie scribbles down a few notes.

1. What did James Brown do before getting into show business?

2. Brown comes from Macon, Georgia. What other famous '50s rocker came from this same city?

3. Who were The Famous Flames?

4. What was Brown's first single?

5. How many number one records did Brown have on the pop charts?

6. Which of these is *not* one of Brown's many self-proclaimed titles? **A.** "Soul Brother #1"; **B.** "The Original Disco Man"; **C.** "The Hardest Working Man In Show Business"; **D.** "Mr. Dynamite."

7. What instruments did Brown play on stage when his band was first starting out?

8. Why did Brown drop out of The Rolling Stones' 1981 tour?

9. In 1969, Brown stood up a big-city mayor who was late for an appointment with him. Name the mayor and the city.

10. Who was known as "The White James Brown?"

11. Who were Nat Kendrick And The Swans, and how did they figure in Brown's career?

12. In the '70s, how much did the I.R.S. claim Brown owed in back taxes?

13. In which of the following films does Brown appear? **A.** *The Blues Brothers;* **B.** *Ski Party;* **C.** *Black Caesar;* **D.** *Slaughter's Big Rip-Off.*

14. Who is the rap/scratch star with whom James Brown recently recorded "Unity"?

15. For what American fast-food giant does Brown now do commercials?

James Brown, the hardest working man in rock.

The Byrds

1. What was The Byrds' original group name?
A. The Beefeaters; **B.** The Sparrows; **C.** The Lime-lighters; **D.** The Hillmen.

2. Name The Byrds' debut single.

3. Another Byrds single was one of the first "psychedelic" songs released. It was also one of the first '60s singles to be banned from airplay. Name it.

4. The Byrds' 1968 album, *Sweetheart Of The Rodeo*, introduced both a new member of the band and a new genre of rock. Name the musician and the style of music he helped usher in.

5. A former child country-music star exerted a strong influence on the band, although he was a member for only a short time. Who was he?

6. Another Byrd left the group to form a seminal country rock outfit. Name the musician and the band.

7. Three other ex-Byrds played with the band of question 6. Who?

8. What fashion accessory did Roger McGuinn and John Lennon help popularize?

9. McGuinn once recorded under a different name. What name did he use?

10. Which Byrd dropped out of the group rather than participate in a South African tour?

11. What is Roger McGuinn's trademark guitar?

12. Which Byrds became members of Dillard & Clark?

13. McGuinn co-wrote "The Chestnut Rose" with a lyricist who later worked with Bob Dylan. Name him.

14. In 1979, McGuinn teamed with what two former Byrds for what album—the title of which carried all three of their names?

15. True or False: Roger McGuinn once worked as Bobby Darin's guitarist in a Las Vegas lounge act.

The Byrds (from left to right): Roger McGuinn, Mike Clark, Chris Hillman, Gene Clarke, David Crosby.

1. At various times, Clapton was a member of Cream, Derek And The Dominos, The Yardbirds, John Mayall's Bluesbreakers, and Blind Faith. Rank these groups from his first to his last.

2. What is Clapton's nickname?

3. What was Cream's first gold single in America?

4. On what Beatles song does Eric Clapton play?

5. Three of rock's greatest guitarists were members of The Yardbirds. Clapton was one. Who preceded him and who followed him?

6. Why did Clapton leave The Yardbirds?

7. In 1966, restroom walls all over London were covered with graffiti about Clapton. What did the graffiti proclaim?

8. Who is "Layla"?

9. What was the name of the band Clapton formed with Steve Winwood, Ginger Baker, and Rick Greach?

10. Eric Clapton's first solo album yielded a hit —a cover of a J.J. Cale tune. Name the song.

11. With what Bob Marley song did Clapton have a #1 hit in 1974?

12. What song did Bob Dylan write for Clapton?

13. What was Clapton's excuse for coming late to his own comeback concert at London's Rainbow Theater in 1973?

14. Clapton was in a film directed by Martin Scorsese. Name it.

15. In 1981, Clapton cancelled his U.S. tour. Why?

Cream (left to right): Eric Clapton, Ginger Baker, Jack Bruce.

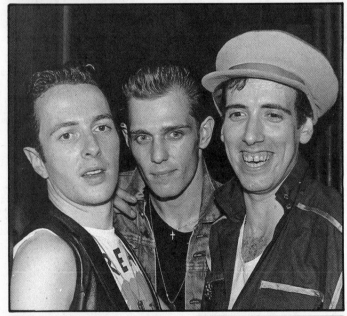

5. Name the original drummer of The Clash.

6. Who named the group, and why?

7. The Clash was a quintet when it debuted. Who was the fifth man?

8. When did the band debut, and what well-known act did they open for?

9. When was The Clash's debut album released in Great Britain?

10. Various band members were charged with illegal possession of firearms. What were they accused of doing with them?

11. When did The Clash first tour America?

12. What was the title of the 1980 film that featured The Clash?

13. Which Clash LP was the first to sell more in the U.S. than in England?

14. When drummer Nicky "Topper" Headon left The Clash in 1982, who replaced him?

15. Which single from the 1982 *Combat Rock* album hit the Top 10 in the U.S.?

1. Joe Strummer was a member of what group prior to The Clash?

2. How did he earn his stage name?

3. What inspired Paul Simonon to take up bass?

4. Mick Jones led another band before forming The Clash. Name the group.

The Clash (left to right): Joe Strummer, Paul Simonon, Mick Jones.   The Clash (left to right): Joe Strummer, Topper Headon, Paul Simonon, Mick Jones.

1. CSN&Y was a reunion for Stephen Stills and Neil Young. In what earlier band had they worked to-gether?

2. Why did David Crosby leave The Byrds?

3. Nash was a former member of what group?

4. What band backed Young after he left Buffalo Springfield but before he joined CSN&Y? What album did they record together?

5. In the late '60s, Young was briefly a member of The Mynah Byrds. What future R&B superstar was also a member?

6. Who was "Long Time Gone" about?

7. Who was the subject of "Suite: Judy Blue Eyes"?

8. "Our House" was based on which trendy co-habiting couple?

9. What incident prompt-ed Young to write "Ohio"?

10. What Joni Mitchell-penned song became a hit for CSN&Y?

11. When did the Y in CSN&Y call it quits?

12. "Heart of Gold" was a hit from Young's only #1 album. Name the album.

13. Which two guitarists appeared on Stills' 1970 debut solo LP?

14. Stills went on to form a new group. What was its name? (Hint: It's also the name of an album.)

15. David Crosby, Stephen Stills, and Graham Nash reunited in 1977 to record the album *CSN*. Name the hit single from the album.

Crosby, Stills, Nash & Young (left to right): David Crosby (with mustache), Neil Young, Stephen Stills, Graham Nash.   Crosby, Stills & Nash (inset).   **15**

THE DOORS

1. Where did the band's founders—singer Jim Morrison and keyboardist Ray Manzarek—meet?

2. Where was the band's name taken from?

3. Jim Morrison published two books of poetry. What were they titled? **A.** *A Feast Of Friends;* **B.** *The Lords And The New Creatures;* **C.** *An American Prayer;* **D.** *No One Here Gets Out Alive.*

4. What (or who) was Morrison's mythical alter ego, and on what album does its name appear?

5. The only concert The Doors ever opened with "When The Music's Over" was also the world's first love-in. Name the gig and the venue where it was held.

6. True or False: The Doors sold more records in 1980 than they did in 1971, the year that *L. A. Woman, Weird Scenes Inside The Gold Mine*, and *Doors 13* were all released.

7. Which of the following Doors albums included the vocals of Jim Morrison? **A.** *Full Circle;* **B.** *The Soft Parade;* **C.** *Other Voices;* **D.** *The Golden Scarab.*

8. What was so unusual about Jim Morrison's relationship with his parents?

9. Why was Morrison jailed for "interfering with the flight of an intercontinental aircraft"?

10. Why was Morrison arrested and jailed in Miami in 1969?

11. For what song were The Doors sued for plagiarism? What British musician brought the suit?

12. What was the name of the band formed in the mid-'70s by former Doors members? **A.** Bobby Krieger And Friends; **B.** Butts Band; **C.** X; **D.** Nite City.

13. A Doors song was used to open a highly controversial, big-budget 1979 war film. Name the film and the song.

14. What famous London restaurant took its name from the flip side of *Morrison Hotel?*

15. How, where, and when did Jim Morrison die? Where is he buried?

1. What was Bob Dylan's real name, when did he change it, and why?

2. Dylan has never had a No. 1 single in the U.S. He *has* had two hits that climbed to No. 2. Name them.

3. On what record did Dylan make his professional debut?

4. When Dylan was 19, his parents paid his way to New York to visit what legendary folk singer?

5. In the early 1960s, Dylan had an intimate relationship with what famous protest singer?

6. For what song did Dylan win his one and only Grammy award?

7. Why was Dylan booed while performing at the 1965 Newport Jazz Festival?

8. What songs were taken off the *The Freewheelin' Bob Dylan* (1963) after the first pressing?

9. What was the name of Dylan's four-hour film opus, a fictionalized account of The Rolling Thunder Revue? In the film, who plays Bob Dylan?

10. Which of the following was *not* a member of Dylan's mid-'70s Rolling Thunder Revue?
A. Sam Shepard; **B.** Allen Ginsburg; **C.** William Burroughs; **D.** Joni Mitchell; **E.** Arlo Guthrie.

11. For what Sam Peckinpah film did Dylan compose the score and play a small part?

12. What well-known poet and author wrote the liner notes for *Desire?*

13. Who received a Grammy for the liner notes on *Blood On The Tracks,* though Dylan had the copy removed from later pressings because he thought the prose too wimpy?

14. What prompted Bob Dylan's 18-month disappearance in the mid-'60s?

15. For what event did Dylan end this self-enforced exile?

Bob Dylan and his one-time girlfriend, Joan Baez.

THE EVERLY BROTHERS

1. Where did The Everly Brothers get their "big break"?

2. True or False: Don and Phil Everly are fraternal twins.

3. Who were the unheralded songwriters responsible for the string of hits (including "Bye Bye Love") that launched the brothers' career?

4. What tune of The Everlys was banned in some areas because of its risqué lyrics?
A. "Wake Up Little Susie";
B. "When Will I Be Loved?"; **C.** "Bye Bye Love"; **D.** "Cathy's Clown."

5. What is the name of the label The Everly Brothers established to "discover and develop new talent"?

6. In 1962, both Don and Phil quit singing for a while to do what?

7. The Everlys toured Britain for the first time in 1970. What noted rock 'n' rollers did they tour with?

8. What was The Everlys' biggest-selling hit?

9. What traumatic event took place at Knott's Berry Farm in July, 1973?

10. When The Everlys first came to Nashville, why were they were hired by country star Roy Acuff?

11. What was the name of The Everlys' TV show? What did it replace?

12. What Everlys song later became a hit for Linda Ronstadt?

13. The Everlys recorded on several labels during their career, including RCA, Warner Bros., Mercury, and Cadence. List the labels in order from earliest to latest.

14. The Everlys came from a show business family. What did their parents do for a living?

15. What two superstars were involved in The Everlys' comeback album?

1. Who are the only original members left in Fleetwood Mac?

2. True or False: Stevie Nicks joined the band after a series of well-publicized auditions were held.

3. What is Christine McVie's maiden name, and what was she doing before she joined Fleetwood Mac?

4. What was Fleetwood Mac's first No. 1 single in America?

5. Which of the following was *never* a Fleetwood Mac guitarist?
A. Bob Weston; **B.** Bob Welch; **C.** Ronnie Lane; **D.** Danny Kirwan; **E.** Lindsey Buckingham.

6. What university marching band took part in a Fleetwood Mac recording, and what was the song?

7. Who did Fleetwood Mac open for on their first U.S. tour?

8. What was so unusual about the departure of founding members Peter Green and Jeremy Spencer?

9. Who managed Fleetwood Mac for most of the '70s and '80s?

10. What do the Bo Street Runners, Peter B's Looners, Shotgun Express, and John Mayall's Bluesbreakers all have in common?

11. Who (or what) was the New Fleetwood Mac?

12. What early Fleetwood Mac album featured the work of blues artists Otis Spann, Willie Dixon, Honeyboy Edwards, and Shakey Horton?

13. Who did Stevie Nicks sing with on "Stop Draggin' My Heart Around" in 1981?

14. Who was the last member to join the group, and when did he/she do it?

15. Where is the Fleetwood Mac star located on the "Hollywood Walk Of Fame"?

Fleetwood Mac (left to right): Lindsey Buckingham, Christine McVie, Mick Fleetwood.

Stevie Nicks of Fleetwood Mac.

MARVIN GAYE

1. Which of the following singers did Gaye *not* record with?
A. Diana Ross; **B.** Tammi Terrell; **C.** Aretha Franklin; **D.** Mary Wells.

2. What was the group Gaye formed in 1957? What was their single?

3. In 1958, Gaye joined what R&B group led by Harvey Fuqua?

4. Gaye was married for 14 years to the sister of what music business legend?

5. What was so unusual about their divorce and settlement?

6. What role did Marvin Gaye play on most of Smokey Robinson's early hits?

7. What is the title of Gaye's "protest" album?

8. What professional sports team did Gaye try out for in 1970?

9. What did Gaye get from Motown to take home and show his father that he was really making it?

10. How did Gaye die?

11. One of Gaye's biggest hits of the '60s opens one of the biggest films of the '80s. Name both.

12. Fill in the blank: "Mercy Mercy Me (___ _____)."

13. Gaye contributed the musical score to which of the following films:
A. *Shaft;* **B.** *Superfly;* **C.** *Trouble Man;* **D.** *Cool Breeze.*

14. What is the title of Gaye's comeback album and final, Grammy-winning single?

15. James Taylor had a hit in 1974 with which Gaye classic?

1. What were The Grateful Dead known as before they changed their tribal moniker to its present one?

2. From where did The Grateful Dead get its name?

3. Jerry Garcia was in several earlier bands. Which *isn't* one of them?
A. Mother McCree's Uptown Jug Champions; **B.** Electric Kool-Aid Acid Test; **C.** Wildwood Boys; **D.** Hart Valley Drifters.

4. Jerry Garcia is missing a finger. Which one is it?

5. What instrument did Jerry Garcia play on Crosby, Stills, Nash & Young's *Déjà Vu* (1970)?

6. What was Jerry Garcia's only spoken line in the film *Gimme Shelter?*

7. What two groups did guitarist Bob Weir form during his stint with The Grateful Dead?

8. True or False: At the start, when The Dead performed in concert, they would have to scrape together a sound system made up of borrowed and stolen sound equipment.

9. Who is "Pigpen," and what ever happened to him?

10. Which Dead album did Lowell George produce?

11. Which of the following groups hired Jerry Garcia to produce their album?
A. New Riders Of The Purple Sage; **B.** Jefferson Airplane; **C.** Diga Rhythm Band; **D.** The Rhythm Devils.

12. How many Top Ten singles have The Dead released?

13. What went wrong with The Dead's early albums *Anthem Of The Sun* ('68) and *Aoxomoxoa* ('69)?

14. Who shared the bill with The Dead at Watkins Glen on July 28, 1973?

15. What connection do The Dead have with noted LSD chemist Owsley Stanley?

The Grateful Dead (left to right): Mickey Hart, Phil Lesh, Bob Weir, Bill Kreutzmann, Ron "Pigpen" McKernan, Jerry Garcia.

JIMI HENDRIX

1. For what rock group did The Jimi Hendrix Experience open on their 1967 U.S. tour?

2. Where was The Jimi Hendrix Experience's first U.S. appearance?

3. What famous rock star introduced the band there?

4. Which act did Hendrix never tour with?
A. Little Richard; B. Solomon Burke; C. Tina Turner.

5. Noel Redding, a member of The Experience, left to form what group?

6. What name did Hendrix and his band use before they became The Experience?

7. What British pop star became Hendrix' manager?

8. Which of his own albums did Hendrix produce?

9. Name the only band for which Hendrix produced an album.

10. In March of 1967, Hendrix did something to his guitar that became a highlight of his act. What did he do?

11. Name Hendrix' highest charting American single.

12. Hendrix played on an album, *You Can Be Anything You Want To Be This Time Around*, that was the project of what '60s guru?

Jimi Hendrix: One of the best guitarists to ever live.

13. Hendrix' flat in London was next door to one that was once inhabited by a famous composer of classical music. Name the composer.

14. What song contains Hendrix' only recorded acoustic guitar work?

15. Who was "Dolly Dagger"?

16. Who backed Hendrix on "Earth Blues"?
A. The Ikettes; **B.** The Marvelettes; **C.** The Ronettes.

17. Procul Harum released a memorial song to Hendrix. Name it.

18. Hendrix recorded an album with a major British guitarist, but the album was never released because the guitarist didn't like the way he sounded. Name the guitarist.

19. What was on the U.K. cover of *Electric Ladyland* but not on the U.S. version?

20. Name two musicians who played with both The Jimi Hendrix Experience and The Band of Gypsies.

21. In 1984, Warner Bros. released a collection of Hendrix hits. What previously unreleased classic is on the album?

22. What do the Symbionese Liberation Army and Jimi Hendrix have in common?

23. How many Hendrix albums were released by Reprise before he died?

24. What jazz keyboardist/arranger produced an album of Hendrix's music after his death?

25. What kind of guitar did Hendrix play?

Jimi Hendrix in the recording studio.

Jimi Hendrix (center) and The Experience.

BUDDY HOLLY

1. Buddy Holly And The Crickets had only one #1 chart topper. It was their first record. Name it.

2. Who owns the entire Buddy Holly song publishing catalog?

3. The Rolling Stones' first American single to make the charts was a cover of a Buddy Holly song. Name it.

4. Who was "Peggy Sue"?

5. True or False: Buddy Holly And The Crickets were one of the first white groups to perform at New York's Apollo Theatre.

6. On February 3, 1959, Holly, The Big Bopper, and Ritchie Valens perished. Where?

7. What ironic noise can be heard at the end of "I'm Gonna Love You, Too"?

8. A member of Holly's band missed the flight, and went on to become a country star in the '70s. Name this outlaw.

9. What Buddy Holly song did not make it on the charts for The Crickets, but was a smash in 1977?

10. Tommy Dee and Carol Kaye commemorated the crash with a song. Name it.

11. Another musician wrote a song in remembrance of Holly titled "Three Steps To Heaven." Name the rockabilly rebel who died soon after he committed this song to vinyl.

12. In the 1970s, Holly was once again commemorated in a song. Name it.

13. Paul Anka wrote Holly's last recorded number. What was it?

14. Match the song with the group who recorded it: 1. Peter And Gordon; 2. Leo Sayer; 3. Santana. **A.** "True Love Ways"; **B.** "Well, All Right"; **C.** "Raining In My Heart."

15. Buddy Holly's life story was presented in a 1978 film. Name the movie and the actor who portrayed Holly.

16. What other well-known act shared the bill at the Surf Ballroom with Buddy Holly And The Crickets, The Big Bopper, and Ritchie Valens that fateful night?

1. List the members of The Jackson 5—Jackie, Jermaine, Marlon, Michael, and Tito—in order from youngest to oldest.

2. Name the other family members to appear on group or solo albums.

3. True or False: The Jacksons wrote and produced most of their material at Motown.

4. Who "discovered" The Jackson 5 and brought them to Motown?
A. Gladys Knight And The Pips; **B.** Diana Ross; **C.** Bobby Taylor; **D.** Berry Gordy, Jr.

5. Who were the first *two* members of the family to release solo albums, and what were they titled?

6. Of what religious order is Michael a member?

7. True or False: Each of The Jackson 5's first six singles reached No. 1.

8. Where did the Jacksons grow up, and where is the Jackson household now?

9. On the day The Jacksons filmed the Pepsi commercial during which Michael's hair caught on fire, what *other* disaster (occurring hours earlier) nearly cancelled the shoot?

10. What unusual stipulation did Michael have written into his $5 million contract with Pepsi?

11. What is the name of Michael's pet boa constrictor?

12. Why did the band change its name from The Jackson 5 to The Jacksons?

13. One of the Jacksons married a record executive's relative. Name the Jackson and his wife.

14. How many Grammy Awards was Michael nominated for in 1984? How many did he win?

15. For whom did he finally take off his sunglasses at the awards presentation?

The Jacksons (left to right, top): Tito, Jackie, Jermaine; (bottom): Michael, Marlon.

JEFFERSON AIRPLANE

9. What was Hot Tuna's original name?

10. When Grace Slick joined Jefferson Airplane, she brought two singles from her former group, The Great Society. Both became Airplane trademarks. Name them.

11. Marty Balin wrote a single for Jefferson Starship that became the biggest selling single either The Starship or The Airplane had ever recorded. Name both the song and the album.

12. What was the title of Grace Slick's 1974 solo album?

13. Who is China?

14. Marty Balin left The Starship and released a solo album in 1981, which spawned a hit single. Name the song and the album.

15. This man, formerly the lead vocalist on the Elvin Bishop hit "Fooled Around And Fell In Love," joined The Starship in 1979. Who is he?

1. Who was Jefferson Airplane's original lead singer?

2. Before joining The Airplane, what did Jack Casady do?

3. What was Papa John Creach's group called?

4. Which Airplane album became the first musical work nominated for the Hugo Award, a science fiction prize?

5. What word did RCA delete from the lyric sheet of *After Bathing At Baxter's* (1967)?

6. Where did Jefferson Airplane play its first show?

7. What then-member of The Byrds wrote "Triad" on *Crown Of Creation?*

8. Spence Dryden left The Airplane for what group?
A. Hot Tuna; **B.** New Riders Of The Purple Sage; **C.** The Sunfighters; **D.** The Matrix.

Jefferson Airplane (from left, clockwise): Paul Kantner, Marty Balin, Jack Casady, Grace Slick, Spencer Dryden, Jorma Kaukonen.   Grace Slick (inset).

1. What is Elton John's real name?

2. *11-17-70* was Elton's first live record. Where was it recorded?

3. What two musicians inspired Elton John's stage name?

4. What was Elton's first major American hit?

5. As of 1974, what is Elton's legal middle name?

6. With which Beatles cover did Elton have a #1 hit?

7. Where and when did Elton John and John Lennon sing onstage together?

8. What do Kiki Dee and Neil Sedaka have in common?

9. How much life insurance did MCA Records take out on Elton in 1974?

10. In 1979, Elton toured Russia and the U.S. with what other musician?

11. Who joined Elton on stage at Madison Square Garden in August of 1982?

12. Who was Elton's "Candle In The Wind" about?

13. In what band did Elton John and Rod Stewart play together?

14. Who is the "someone" in "Someone Saved My Life"?

15. Name the #1 hit that Elton recorded with Kiki Dee.

Elton John, one of the biggest stars of the '70s.

JANIS JOPLIN

4. What did Janis Joplin, Bob Dylan, and Todd Rundgren have in common?

5. What was Joplin's only #1 hit?

6. Big Brother And The Holding Company had a Top 20 hit in 1968. Name it.

7. What was Joplin referring to when she said: "I can't go out the same year because he's a bigger star"?

8. What song was released as an instrumental because Joplin died before writing the lyrics?

9. What did Joplin drink on stage during concerts?

10. What Hollywood film was loosely based on the life of Janis Joplin?

11. What Joplin-penned song, released after her death, was about a car?

12. What member of Big Brother also played in Joplin's Full-Tilt Boogie Band?

13. Joplin became a superstar after performing at what rock concert?

1. Who was Pearl?

2. What were the names of Joplin's three bands?

3. What was tattooed on Joplin's wrist?

14. List these albums featuring Joplin in order of release from first to last. **A.** *Cheap Thrills*; **B.** *Big Brother And The Holding Company*; **C.** *Pearl*; **D.** *I Got Dem Ol' Kozmic Blues Again*.

　Janis Joplin (second from left) and Big Brother And The Holding Company (inset).　　The best white blues singer of the '60s: Janis Joplin.

1. List these Kinks albums in order of release, from earliest to latest.
A. *Sleepwalker*; B. *Everybody's In Showbiz*; C. *Give The People What They Want*; D. *Kinda Kinks*.

2. "The Kinks" was the second name the band worked under. What was the first?

3. What is the title of The Kinks' 1969 rock opera?

4. What was Dave Davies' first British solo hit?

5. The Kinks recorded one of the first songs to deal with transvestism. Name the song and the album it appeared on.

6. What word did Ray Davies have to re-record on "Lola" because of a copyright infringement?

7. What record label did The Kinks own?

8. What hard-rock group had a hit with The Kinks' "You Really Got Me" in 1978?

9. What new-wave group recorded "Stop Your Sobbin'" in 1978?

10. The Kinks produced one of the first full-length rock videos, taken from footage of a North American tour. Name the video.

11. With what well-known rock star did Ray Davies father a child?

12. What was unusual about the title of Dave Davies' first solo album?

13. Which of the following films did Ray Davies score?
A. *Percy*; B. *Jubilee*; C. *David Watts*; D. *Virgin Soldiers*.

14. What did Ray Davies do for a living before he became a musician?

The Kinks (clockwise from top left): Peter Quaife, Ray Davies, Dave Davies, Mick Avory.

Ray Davies of The Kinks.

KISS

6. What was unusual about the printing of Marvel Comics' special Kiss comic book?

7. How long is Gene Simmons' tongue?

8. Who co-starred with Kiss in *Kiss Meets The Phantom*, a 1978 made-for-TV movie? In what setting did the movie take place?

9. Which of these would *not* be considered normal concert behavior for Gene Simmons?
A. biting off the head of a live bird; **B.** spitting fire; **C.** drooling blood; **D.** sticking his tongue out.

10. What unusual sales strategy did the band undertake in 1978? Was it successful?

11. On what album cover did Kiss reveal their faces for the first time?

12. What avant-garde rocker helped write the concept album *Music From "The Elder"* (1981)?

13. What reason did drummer Peter Criss give for leaving the band?

14. His replacement was given a new makeup concept. What was it?

15. True or False: The band was more successful in England than in any other country.

1. The group was founded by Gene Simmons and Paul Stanley. What was the name of their earlier band?

2. How did they recruit the other original two members of the band?

3. What was Gene Simmons doing for a living when the band got started?

4. Which band member's makeup looked like a cat? Who had a large star painted over his right eye?

5. Which of the following *never* played guitar with Kiss?
A. Ace Frehley; **B.** Eric Carr; **C.** Vinny Vincent; **D.** Mark St. John.

1. What famous rock 'n' roll drummer gave Led Zeppelin its name?

2. Who did Led Zeppelin open for on its first American tour?

3. All four members of the soon-to-be-formed Led Zeppelin played on what British singer's *Three Weeks Hero* album (1968)?

4. Where did the band's founders — guitarist Jimmy Page and bass player John Paul Jones — meet?

5. Who were Page's and Jones' *original* choices to round out Led Zeppelin?

6. How long did it take to record the band's first album?
A. 9 hours; **B.** 30 hours;
C. 4 days; **D.** 4 months.

7. Who recommended Robert Plant to the group?

8. What was Led Zeppelin's only Top Ten hit?
A. "Stairway To Heaven";
B. "Whole Lotta Love";
C. "Immigrant Song";
D. "No Quarter."

9. Why was the massive popularity of "Stairway To Heaven" so unusual?

10. The definitive Led Zeppelin concert movie was released in 1976 — what is its title?

11. How many different album covers did *In Through The Out Door* (1979) have?

12. What was so unusual about the album sleeve for *Physical Graffiti* (1975)?

13. What was the name of Jimmy Page's first solo LP?

14. Name Robert Plant's two solo albums, and the label they were recorded for.

15. Robert Plant and Jimmy Page recently teamed up for an album of blues and early rock 'n' roll. Name the group and their debut album.

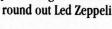

Robert Plant (inset).

Led Zeppelin (left to right): John Paul Jones, Jimmy Page, John Bonham, Robert Plant.

LITTLE RICHARD

8. Little Richard gave up rock 'n' roll (for religion) for the first time on an Australian tour. How did he "prove" his faith that day?

9. Little Richard shared the bill with The Doors, Bo Diddley, and Jerry Lee Lewis at what music festival?

10. Name the 1971 album on which Little Richard appears with members of Canned Heat and such '60s lights as Harvey Mandel and Charles Lloyd.

11. At 13, Little Richard moved in with a white couple, Ann and Enotris Johnson. How did Mr. Johnson most figure in Little Richard's rise to stardom?

12. What was the name of Little Richard's own traveling band?

13. When Little Richard went into the ministry in 1958, what singer took over this band?

14. In what church was Little Richard ordained a minister?

15. True or False: After Little Richard became a preacher, he gave up rock 'n' roll for gospel music.

1. What is Little Richard's *last* name?

2. How old was Richard when he cut his first singles; what major label were they on?

3. Who was his manager (and frequent co-writer) during his "glory years"?

4. Where were his classic string of hits recorded, and for what label?

5. Name the four classic Little Richard hits covered by Elvis Presley in 1956.

6. Little Richard was the first inspiration (as well as an early boss) of what '60s psychedelic star?

7. In which of the following 1950s films did Little Richard *not* appear?
A. *The Girl Can't Help It*;
B. *Rock Rock Rock*; **C.** *Mr. Rock And Roll*; **D.** *Knock The Rock*.

1. Bob Marley frequently wrote songs about what earthly leader, to whom his religion ascribed heavenly powers?

2. What influence did schoolmates Winston Hubert McIntosh and Neville O'Reiley Livingstone have on Marley's career?

3. What is the title of the first Wailers LP released in the U.S.?
A. *Judge Not*; **B.** *Simmer Down*; **C.** *Catch A Fire*; **D.** *Exodus*.

4. Name a Bob Marley song that was later a hit for Eric Clapton.

5. By what name were Marley's label and studio operations collectively known?

6. Why did Bunny Wailer leave The Wailers?

7. Which was the only song sung by The Wailers to make the U.S. Top 100 charts?

8. What political feat did Marley accomplish at the "One Love Peace Concert" held in Kingston, Jamaica during the late '70s?

9. Who did Bob Marley And The Wailers back on their first major U.S. tour?

10. In 1979, The Wailers played at the Inaugural Ball of what new African nation?

11. What two British superstars signed ex-Wailer Peter Tosh in 1978, and sat in on an a cover of the Motown classic, "Don't Look Back"?

12. True or False: During a low ebb in his career, Marley once took a job in a Delaware auto factory.

13. What American singer had a No. 1 British hit with Marley's "Stir It Up"?

14. After Wailer and Tosh left, whom did Marley bring in as replacements?

15. True or False: Marley was assassinated by right-wing extremists opposed to his political views.

JONI MITCHELL

1. What was the first instrument Joni Mitchell learned to play?

2. Where is Mitchell from, and what was her maiden name?

3. When she enrolled at college she intended to become:
A. a musician; **B.** a politician; **C.** an artist; **D.** an undertaker.

4. Who produced Mitchell's debut album?

5. Who was "A Free Man In Paris"?

6. Did Mitchell play at the Woodstock Festival?

7. Match the song with the artist(s) who popularized it:
1. "Woodstock"; 2. "Both Sides Now"; 3. "The Circle Game"; 4. "Eastern Rain."
A. Tom Rush; **B.** Fairport Convention; **C.** Judy Collins; **D.** CSN&Y.

8. What jazz bassist did Joni once team up with?

9. Mitchell's affairs with three of the four members of what group once earned her *Rolling Stone's* "Old Lady Of The Year" award?

10. Who did Mitchell write "The Circle Game" for?

11. Jaco Pastorius, Michael Brecker, Pat Metheny, and The Persuasions accompanied Mitchell on which album?

12. True or False: "Big Yellow Taxi" (1970) was Mitchell's only No. 1 hit on the U.S. charts.

13. What special relationship does Mitchell enjoy with her bass player?

14. Who did the painting on the cover of *Wild Things Run Fast* (1982)?

15. What did someone shout at 1970's Isle of Wight Festival that made Mitchell cry?

1. Where did the trio form?

2. Paul Stookey already had stage experience when he joined the group. What was his other talent?

3. When did they release their debut album, and for what label?

4. What was Peter, Paul & Mary's first Top Ten smash?

5. Who were the founding fathers of folk who wrote the group's first hit?

6. The trio struck gold twice with covers of songs by what young folk singer? What were the songs?

7. Why was "Puff, The Magic Dragon" so controversial?

8. Who wrote the trio's #1 hit, "Leaving On A Jet Plane"?

9. Which Peter, Paul & Mary song featured skillful imitations of The Beatles, Donovan, and The Mamas And The Papas?

10. In 1967, the trio released an album called *Album 1700*. What did the title represent?

11. When did they initially call it quits as a trio?

12 What were the titles of their three solo LPs, issued in 1971?

13. Why did Peter Yarrow serve three months in prison in 1970?

14. Paul Stookey has found solo fame recording what sort of music?

15. Yarrow co-wrote and co-produced what 1977 smash for Mary McGregor?

PINK FLOYD

12. For which ex-Soft Machine member did Mason produce an album in 1974?

13. David Gilmour played guitar on a 1984 Paul McCartney song. Name the song.

1. Which of the following was not an original member of Pink Floyd? **A.** David Gilmour; **B.** Nick Mason; **C.** Roger Waters; **D.** Richard Wright.

2. *Dark Side Of The Moon* (1973) is still on the Billboard Top 200 album charts over ten years after its release. What album previously held the longevity record?

3. What Pink Floyd album was supported by a tour that featured a flying pig?

4. What is the title of Pink Floyd's debut album?

5. Who is "Shine On You Crazy Diamond" about?

6. Pink Floyd was the first rock group to perform at what prestigious classical festival?

7. What Hyde Park rock tradition did Pink Floyd start?

8. What is the origin of the group's name?

9. What four sound tracks did Pink Floyd score between 1969 and 1972?

10. True or False: Pink Floyd was the first group to use digital sound in concert.

11. "Another Brick In The Wall" was banned by what government in 1980?

14. Pink Floyd's first two albums were later re-released as a set under what title? What were the names of the two albums it encompassed?

15. In 1973, Harvest Records sent out a cleaned-up version of the song "Money." What offensive word was changed?

Pink Floyd (clockwise from top left): Nick Mason, Syd Barrett, Richard Wright, Roger Waters.   **David Gilmour of Pink Floyd (inset).**

1. Which of the following bands did Andy Summers never play in?
A. Eric Burdon And The Animals; **B.** The Kevin Ayers Band; **C.** John Mayall's Bluesbreakers; **D.** The Neil Sedaka Band.

2. Who is the only American member of The Police?

3. Before forming The Police, of what British progressive rock group was Stewart Copeland a member?

4. What was the group's first American Top 40 hit?

5. Who is Klark Kent?

6. Before he became a professional musician, how did Sting earn his living?

7. Match the single with the album: 1. *Regatta De Blanc*; 2. *Outlandos D'Amour*; 3. *Zenyatta Mondatta*; 4. *Synchronicity*.

8. Which member of the group is a natural blond?

9. Who was The Police's first guitarist?

10. What is Sting's real name?

A. "So Lonely"; **B.** "Message In A Bottle"; **C.** "King Of Pain"; **D.** "Driven To Tears."

11. Stewart Copeland's brothers, Miles and Ian, are the heads of a record label and a booking agency, respectively. Name these two companies.

12. What Police single won a Grammy for "Song Of The Year" in 1983?

13. Summers collaborated with Robert Fripp on two albums. Can you name one?

14. What Francis Coppola movie did Copeland score?

15. What book inspired Sting to write the song "Don't Stand So Close To Me"?

The Police (left to right): Stewart Copeland, Sting, Andy Summers.

Sting, Stewart Copeland, Andy Summers (inset).

ELVIS PRESLEY

1. In 1955, Presley auditioned for *Arthur Godfrey's Talent Scouts* but was rejected. Who won?

2. What was Presley's first single release?

3. Who first recorded "Are You Lonesome Tonight?"

4. Who were the members of Presley's original backup band, The Blue Moon Boys?

5. Name the members of the "Million Dollar Quartet."

6. On what TV show did Presley croon "Hound Dog" to a bassett hound?

7. What Carl Perkins song did Elvis have a hit with?

8. In 1956, a Presley single was the first to make the pop, R&B, and C&W charts simultaneously. Name that tune.

9. Before he began recording, what did Presley do for a living?

10. In December of 1960, five "answer songs" were released in response to an Elvis hit. Name it.

11. Presley released the first LP ever that did not have the star's name on the front cover. Name it.

12. Presley recorded a Simon & Garfunkel song in 1970. Name it.

13. Presley recorded two Bob Dylan songs. Name them.

14. What James Taylor song did Presley record in 1973?

15. Match the movie with the name of Presley's character: 1. *Love Me Tender;* 2. *Loving You;* 3. *King Creole;* 4. *Blue Hawaii* **A.** Deke Rivers; **B.** Clint Reno; **C.** Chad Gates; **D.** Danny Fisher.

16. In what movie did Presley co-star with Walter Matthau?

17. In 1973, Presley appeared in the first satellite-broadcast TV concert. Name the program.

Elvis reveals a touch of his famous sneer.

18. What contemporary country superstar penned "Kentucky Rain"?

19. On what Memphis label, known for its rockabilly artists, did Presley debut in July of 1954?

20. Who wrote or co-wrote "Don't Be Cruel," "All Shook Up," and "Return To Sender" for Presley but never met him?

21. Who did the original "Hound Dog" in 1952?

22. What peculiar marketing ploy did RCA employ in September, 1956?

23. What Presley hit was written specifically for his 1968 TV special, *Singer Presents Elvis?*

24. A well-known Presley clone scored a #19 hit in June of 1961 with a tune from Elvis' first post-army LP. Name him.

25. What was the first song Presley recorded?

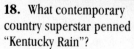
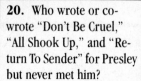
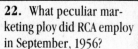
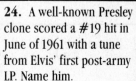

Elvis Presley in a stunning production number from his 1957 movie, *Jailhouse Rock.* 39

PRINCE

5. Which of these solo artists is *not* a former member of Prince's "Purple Kingdom" entourage? **A.** Vanity; **B.** Dez Dickerson; **C.** Francis L.; **D.** Morris Day.

6. What was so noteworthy about Prince's video for his hit, "Little Red Corvette" (1982)?

7. What do the initials in Prince's "D.M.S.R." stand for?

8. In 1978, Prince assembled five local musicians to back him in concert. Of these, how many are in his current touring band, The Revolution?

9. Who is Jamie Starr?

10. What was the *original* title of the movie *Purple Rain?*

11. In *Purple Rain,* what is the name of the club where "The Kid" performs? Where is it located?

1. True or False: Prince's *real* name is "Prince."

2. What demand did Warner Bros. Records meet when they signed Prince in 1978? How old was Prince at the time?

3. What unusual feat did Prince pull off on his debut album?

4. Which Prince song did Chaka Khan turn into a hit in 1984? What album did it first appear on?

12. Who are D.D. Winters and Patty Kotero, and how were they involved in the making of *Purple Rain?*

13. In the film, where does The Kid tell Apollonia to purify herself?

14. "When Doves Cry" simultaneously reached No. 1 on which *three* of *Billboard's* charts?

15. What was Sheila E. doing before she was "discovered" by Prince?

His Royal Badness, Prince.

1. Under what name did The Velvet Underground first record?

2. True or False: Pop artist Peter Max was instrumental in the band's early success.

3. List the order (from first to last) that the five founders of The Velvet Underground—Lou Reed, John Cale, Nico, Sterling Morrison, and Maureen Tucker—left the band.

4. The first Velvet Underground album was dedicated to what noted poet (also one of Reed's professors at Syracuse)?

5. What was Lou Reed's only Top 20 hit?

6. On what album does this single appear; who co-produced this album?

7. What was unusual about the cover of The Velvet Underground's first album?

8. What did John Cale do at a recital at the Guild Hall School Of Music—where he was a classical music student—that gave him early notoriety?

9. Which band member became an English teacher at a Texas university?

10. After Reed left The Velvet Underground, what did he briefly do for a living?

11. In what magazine did Lou Reed once publish his poetry?

12. What bit of theatrics would Reed go through when performing "Heroin"?

13. What was the Exploding Plastic Inevitable?

14. Critics mercilessly blasted Reed's *Metal Machine Music* (1975). What was RCA's reaction?

15. In which of the following films did Reed make a cameo appearance?
A. *The Blues Brothers;* B. *Pink Floyd's The Wall;* C. *Fame;* D. *One-Trick Pony;* E. *Purple Rain.*

THE ROLLING STONES

1. What do Dick Taylor, Mick Avory, Tony Chapman, and Ian Stewart have in common?

2. Where did Mick Jagger and Keith Richards meet for the first time?

3. Match The Stones' first four singles with the artists who originally wrote and/ or popularized them: 1. "Come On"; 2. "I Wanna Be Your Man"; 3. "Not Fade Away"; 4. "It's All Over Now."

A. John Lennon and Paul McCartney; **B.** Buddy Holly; **C.** Chuck Berry; **D.** Bobby Womack And The Valentinos.

4. What was The Rolling Stones' first No. 1 hit in America? In England?

5. What was the pseudonym used by The Rolling Stones on their early group compositions?

6. Ed Sullivan once asked The Stones to censor the lyrics to a song they were planning to sing on his show. What was the song?

7. Where did The Rolling Stones get their name?

8. What Stones song featured Paul McCartney and John Lennon on backing vocals?

9. On what Carly Simon song does Mick Jagger sing backup vocals?

The Rolling Stones (left to right, top): Keith Richards, Brian Jones, Bill Wyman; (bottom): Charlie Watts, Mick Jagger.

13. True or False: Director Steven Spielberg was hired as a cameraman for that famous concert.

14. For what other singer did Jagger and Richards write "As Tears Go By"?

15. True or False: At the time of his death, guitarist Brian Jones had already quit The Stones and been replaced.

16. What was Jagger's public tribute to Jones?

17. Early in their career, The Rolling Stones opened for this soulful singer/songwriter. Later, he opened for The Stones. Name him.

20. Which of the following films feature Mick Jagger in a dramatic role?
A. *Performance* (1970);
B. *Fitzcarraldo* (1983);
C. *One Plus One* (1968);
D. *Ned Kelly* (1970).

21. Who designed The Stones' "licking tongue" corporate logo, and where did it first appear?

22. What famed reggae artist was signed by The Stones' private label?

23. Which of the following is *not* one of The Stones' live albums?
A. *Got Live If You Want It* (1969); **B.** *Still Life (1982);* **C.** *Goat's Head Soup (1973);* **D.** *Get Yer Ya-Yas Out* (1970).

10. On the *Flowers* album cover, each band member's face appears in an oval on a stem of a flower. What was different about Brian Jones' flower?

11. What was the name of the feature-length documentary about The Stones' 1969 tour?

12. What one outdoor concert was featured extensively? And why?

18. What was pictured on *Beggar's Banquet* ('68) before it was cleaned up?

19. What famous women peered out of the cut-outs on the uncensored version of the *Some Girls* cover?

24. Where did Jagger go to record his long-awaited solo album *She's The Boss* (1985)?

25. Who were The New Barbarians?

Mick Jagger of The Rolling Stones.

The Rolling Stones (left to right): Bill Wyman, Ron Wood, Mick Jagger, Keith Richards.

ROXY MUSIC

1. Name Roxy Music's original synthesist.

2. Who produced the group's first album?

3. What Roxy member later helped form UK?

4. Roxy Music enjoyed only modest success in America. Name their only two singles to reach the Top 30.

5. The European cover of 1974's *Country Life* sported two scantily clad women. What was on most American versions?

6. What two albums were released while Roxy Music was officially disbanded?

7. What two musicians have been in both Roxy Music and King Crimson?

8. What do Rik Kenton, John Porter, Graham Simpson, Sal Maida, John Gustafson, John Wetton, Gary Tibbs, Alan Spenner, and Rick Wills all have in common?

9. With whom did Brian Eno team for the legendary *June 1, 1974* album?

10. Who did Eno collaborate with on *No Pussyfooting* and *Evening Star* (both 1973)?

11. What unusual concert costume did Bryan Ferry wear in the '70s?

12. What future Rolling Stones paramour dated Bryan Ferry in the '70s?

13. Match the Roxy member with his solo album: 1. Brian Eno; 2. Bryan Ferry; 3. Phil Manzanera. **A.** *Listen Now* (1977); **B.** *Music For Films* (1977); **C.** *The Bride Stripped Bare* (1978).

14. "2 H.B." was recorded by both Roxy Music and Bryan Ferry. To whom is the song dedicated?

15. Roxy Music had a No. 1 British hit with which John Lennon song?

44   Bryan Ferry of Roxy Music.

Roxy Music (left to right): Andy McKay, Bryan Ferry, Phil Manzanera.

1. What was this duo's name before they went by their real names? What was their "hit" 1957 single?

2. Where did Simon & Garfunkel first meet and sing together?

3. Which one of the following names did Paul Simon *not* record under? **A.** Paul Kane; **B.** Jerry Landis; **C.** Arty Garr; **D.** Tico And The Triumphs.

4. What Simon & Garfunkel tune, first released as an all-acoustic number, went on to become a hit after the producer added drums and electric instruments to the mix?

5. For what movie sound track did Simon & Garfunkel do an album of songs?

6. What was Paul Simon's only No. 1 solo single?

7. In what Woody Allen film does Paul Simon have a minor role?

8. Name the 1980 film that Paul Simon wrote, starred in, and composed the sound track for.

9. In which (if any) of these films do *neither* Paul Simon nor Art Garfunkel appear? **A.** *Carnal Knowledge;* **B.** *This Is Spinal Tap;* **C.** *Catch-22;* **D.** *Bad Timing.*

10. Where did Simon & Garfunkel stage their 1981 reunion concert?

11. The duo also reteamed for what 1972 benefit? (Peter, Paul & Mary also reunited for it.)

12. True or False: Art Garfunkel has never had a Top 10 hit as a solo artist.

13. What was the biggest selling single and album ever recorded by the duo?

14. What song appeared on solo albums by both Simon and Garfunkel?

15. What 1978 single featured the three-part harmony of Simon, Garfunkel, and James Taylor?

Paul Simon

SLY AND THE FAMILY STONE

1. What is Sly's real name?

2. What did Sly do before he became a performer?

3. What 1964 dance hit by Bobby Freeman did Sly produce?

4. He also produced a #15 hit for a Bay area group. Who were they, and what was the tune?

5. Before they became The Family Stone, what was Sly's band called?

6. What did Sly play?

7. What was their debut single?

8. Name their first Top Ten hit.

9. What was the band's first release to hit #1 on both the pop and R&B charts?

10. What was their last release to do the same?

11. Where did Sly marry Kathy Silva in 1974?

12. What was Sly's brother Freddie's job with the band?

13. Which group member went on to record many '70s R&B hits, and what was the name of his group?

14. Sly toured with another funk pioneer in the early '80s. Who?

15. Sly did something during a free concert in Chicago that led to a lengthy ban on free outdoor rock concerts in the city. What did he do?

Sly And The Family Stone (left to right): Rose Stone, Larry Graham, Sly, Freddie Stone, Jerry Martini, Gregg Enrico, Cynthia Robinson. **Sly Stone**

7. In 1977, Ronnie Spector had a comeback hit with a song written by Billy Joel. Name it.

8. All of the following are by The Crystals except:
A. "Da Doo Ron Ron"; **B.** "He's Sure The Boy I Love"; **C.** "Then He Kissed Me"; **D.** "Walking In The Rain."

9. What Beatles album did Spector produce?

10. Who sang "River Deep, Mountain High"?

11. Spector belonged to a group that had a hit song based on an inscription on Spector's father's tombstone. Name the song and the group.

12. Spector plays acoustic guitar on what Rolling Stones song?

13. What is the name of the style of sound recording that Spector developed?

1. Name two Ronettes hits with the word "baby" in their titles.

2. A backup singer with The Ronettes went on to become a big star. Who is she?

3. What is the original name of the Phil Spector Christmas LP?

4. "Walking In The Rain" was a big hit for which of the following:
A. The Marvelettes; **B.** The Ronettes; **C.** The Shangri-Las; **D.** Shirley and Lee.

5. What is the name of the record label Spector started?

6. Phil and Ronnie Spector had a baby boy. What is his name?

14. Spector served as a consultant to what major benefit rock concert?

15. Spector played the role of a dope pusher in what '60s movie?

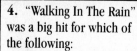

The boy wonder, Phil Spector.

The Ronettes (top to bottom): Estelle Bennett, Nedra Talley, Ronnie Bennett Spector (inset).

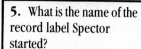

Tina Turner (inset).   47

BRUCE SPRINGSTEEN

1. Who did Bruce Springsteen And The E Street Band open for on their first major Northeast tour?

2. What was Springsteen's first Top Ten hit?

3. In April, 1976, Springsteen tried unsuccessfully to enter Graceland to visit his idol, Elvis Presley. What did he tell the guards in hopes of gaining entrance?

4. Who said "I saw the future of rock 'n' roll, and his name is Bruce Springsteen"?

5. What is Bruce's nickname? Clarence Clemons'?

6. Who did Springsteen open for at the Schaeffer Music Festival in New York City in August, 1974? **A.** Anne Murray; **B.** Ike And Tina Turner; **C.** The Hollies; **D.** The New York Dolls.

7. What Springsteen song did Patti Smith have a hit with?

8. What contribution did Springsteen make to Lou Reed's *Street Hassle?*

9. Who replaced Miami Steve in The E Street Band?

10. Who recorded "Elmer Fudd Sings Bruce Springsteen"?

11. What famous film director directed the "Dancing In The Dark" video?

12. What is unusual about the video for "Atlantic City"?

13. Match the song with the album: 1. *The River;* 2. *Born To Run;* 3. *Nebraska;* 4. *Born In The U.S.A.* **A.** "Cover Me"; **B.** "Thunder Road"; **C.** "Atlantic City"; **D.** "Independence Day."

Clarence Clemons and Bruce Springsteen do the hula (inset).

14. Where was "the little girlie with the blue jeans so tight" riding through?

15. Name four Springsteen songs that have cars in the titles.

16. Why was it Rosalita's last chance?

17. Who had a #1 hit with "Blinded By The Light"?

18. In "Jungleland," what does Springsteen call the local cops?

19. In what Martin Scorsese film did Clarence Clemons perform?

20. What book is "Darkness On The Edge Of Town" based on?

21. Springsteen and Miami Steve co-produced a comeback album for what famous early rocker?

22. Miami Steve left The E Street Band to form his own group. Name it.

23. What was unusual about the album *Nebraska?*

24. Who said "Baby, if you want to be wild, you've got a lot to learn"?

25. "Born To Run" is sung to a girl. What is her name?

Bruce Springsteen in concert. 49

ROD STEWART

1. What Stewart album was No. 1 in the U.S. and the U.K. simultaneously, the first LP ever to occupy both slots at the same time?

2. Before he joined The Faces, Stewart was a member of what band?

3. What was the original title of *The Rod Stewart Album?*

4. What happened when Rod Stewart and Ron Wood joined The Small Faces?

5. What Scandinavian movie star did Stewart live with?

6. Name the members of The Faces.

7. How did Stewart earn a living before becoming a professional musician?

8. When Stewart signed his first contract as a solo artist, he received no money. What *did* he get?

9. How did Stewart contribute to Millie Small's #2 hit, "My Boy, Lollipop"?

10. Who wrote "Angel" on Stewart's *Never A Dull Moment?*

11. Who wrote Stewart's smash, "The First Cut Is The Deepest"?

12. Name Stewart's sexy 1979 #1 hit.

13. What has Stewart been known to do to prevent panty-lines from showing through his tight-fitting trousers?

14. In 1973, Stewart responded to a $12.5 million palimony suit by Britt Ekland by dedicating a song to her. What is the song's title?

15. Match the single with the album: 1. *Every Picture Tells A Story;* 2. *A Night On The Town;* 3. *Foolish Behavior;* 4. *Camouflage.*

A. "Passion"; **B.** "Maggie May"; **C.** "Infatuation"; **D.** "Tonight's The Night."

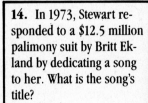

A natty young Rod Stewart.

1. Name the 1979 hit that featured a duet between Summer and Barbra Streisand.

2. What was Summer's first major show biz break?

3. Who produced her early hits?

4. Where were her early recordings made?

5. What was Summer's first U.S. hit?

6. What was her first No. 1 pop hit?

7. Who was the well-known actor who hit with that song before Summer?

8. Its songwriter is equally well known. Name him.

9. Summer appeared in what disco-oriented flick in 1978?

10. Which song from the movie sound track won Summer a Grammy?

11. She scored a pair of No. 1 pop hits on her 1980 *Bad Girls* LP. What were they?

12. Who did she marry in 1980?

13. Who produced her 1982 album, *Donna Summer?*

14. Who wrote "Protection" for Donna for her '82 album *Donna Summer?*

THE SUPREMES

3. Name the three original members of the group.

4. To what label did Diana Ross defect when she left Motown in 1981?

5. Who was the first "replacement" Supreme?

6. What girl group did this replacement come from?

7. Who replaced Ross when she left the group?

8. Name the producing/songwriting trio that created many of the early Supremes hits.

9. Name three movies Ross starred in.

10. What Ross hit did Michael Jackson write?

11. What Supremes survivor formed a spinoff of The Supremes?

1. What was The Supremes' original name? **A.** The Primettes; **B.** The Marvelettes; **C.** The Divines; **D.** The Kittens.

12. What was the last Diana Ross And The Supremes hit?

13. What 1968 hit did The Supremes record with The Temptations?

2. The three members of the group were from the same ghetto area. Name it.

14. Rank these Ross solo albums in order of release from earliest to latest: **A.** *Why Do Fools Fall In Love;* **B.** *Ross;* **C.** *Silk Electric;* **D.** *Mahogany.*

The Supremes (left to right): Florence Ballard, Diana Ross, Mary Wilson.

The glamorous Diana Ross.

1. Where did David Byrne and Chris Frantz meet?

2. What was Byrne and Frantz' first band together?

3. Who did the Talking Heads tour Europe with before recording their first album?

4. Tina Weymouth's three sisters are in The Tom Tom Club. Name them.

5. What Al Green song did the Heads have a hit with?

6. Who produced *Remain In Light?*

7. What B-52s album did Byrne produce?

8. Who designed the limited-edition cover art for *Speaking In Tongues?*

9. Which members of the band are married to each other?

10. What former member of Labelle served as a Talking Heads vocalist?

11. What is the name of the Talking Heads' concert film?

12. With which album did the group begin experimenting with African performance techniques?

13. What two Heads formed their own band in 1981?

14. Byrne wrote a score for Twyla Tharp. What album contained the highlights of the piece?

15. What was the band's first major video and who choreographed it?

David Byrne of Talking Heads.

Tina Weymouth of Talking Heads. 53

THE WHO

1. Why does Roger Daltrey stutter on "My Generation"?

2. Why was "My Generation" banned by the BBC?

3. A punk group recorded a satirical reply to "My Generation" in 1978. Name the group and the single.

4. Name The Who's only U.S. Top Ten single.

5. The Who's debut single featured a ubiquitous session player. Name the single and the guitarist.

6. The Who earned an entry in the Guinness Book Of World Records. How?

7. What was The Who called in the early days? **A.** The High Numbers; **B.** The Detours; **C.** The Face; **D.** The Daltrey Gang.

8. Who was Pete Townshend's guru?

9. On November 20, 1973, Keith Moon collapsed on stage in San Francisco. How did the show go on?

10. On what LP did The Who first experiment with synthesizers?

11. Based on the cover of *The Who Sell Out,* match the prop with the star: 1. Moon; 2. Entwhistle; 3. Daltrey; 4. Townshend. **A.** Baked beans; **B.** A bottle of deodorant; **C.** A teddy bear; **D.** Acne cream.

12. Which of the following is not an Entwhistle LP? **A.** *Mad Dog;* **B.** *So What?;* **C.** *Whistle Rhymes;* **D.** *Smash Your Head Against The Wall.*

13. Who was John Browne?

14. What word was spelled out on the football helmets on the cover of *Odds And Sods?*

15. Name four films in which Roger Daltrey appeared.

Pete Townshend of The Who.   The Who (left to right): Roger Daltrey, John Entwhistle, Pete Townshend, Keith Moon.   Roger Daltrey of The Who.

16. Destroying their instruments after a concert was an early Who tradition. How did the practice start?

17. What was The Who's first Townshend-penned single?

18. What's the only composition credited to both Townshend and Daltrey?

19. The windmill guitar-playing style is a Townshend trademark. Who did Townshend believe he was imitating?

20. What motel chain banned The Who from ever returning after a particularly boisterous Keith Moon birthday party?

21. What country did The Who vow never to tour again after an especially grueling visit in 1968?

22. Who drew the cover of *The Who By Numbers?*

23. What alias did Keith Moon use when he appeared on John Lennon's *Sometime In New York City?*

24. In what Eric Burdon And The Animals song is The Who mentioned by name?

25. Pete Townshend released a solo album in 1980. Name it and the Top Ten single it spawned.

The Who (left to right): John Entwhistle, Roger Daltrey, Pete Townshend, Keith Moon. 55

STEVIE WONDER

1. What is Stevie Wonder's real name?

2. What group opened for Wonder's 1964 British tour, and then had Wonder open for them on their U.S. tour eight years later?

3. On what album did Wonder play all the instruments except saxophone and one guitar solo?

4. What album had liner notes printed in Braille?

5. What multi-octave singer had a #1 single produced by Wonder?

6. Name the hairdo Wonder popularized that was later adopted by Cher and Bo Derek.

7. What lingering damage did Wonder sustain after his 1975 car accident?

8. What Bob Dylan song did Wonder have a hit with?

9. What British guitarist appeared on "Looking For Another Pure Love" on the *Talking Book* LP?

10. Wonder first hit the charts with what tune?

11. In 1964, Wonder appeared in two films. Name them.

12. What 1977 film did Wonder score?

13. Match the hit with the album: 1. *Hotter Than July*; 2. *Songs In The Key Of Life*; 3. *Talking Book*; 4. *Uptight*.

A. "Sir Duke"; **B.** "Master Blaster (Jammin')"; **C.** "For Once In My Life"; **D.** "Superstition."

14. Wonder hit the charts in 1984 with yet another No. 1 hit. Name it.

15. A Stevie Wonder/ Paul McCartney duet made it to No. 1 in 1982. Name that tune.

1. What did Frank Zappa's father do for a living?

2. What atypical "classical" piece did a young Frank Zappa perform on *The Steve Allen Show?*

3. Who are Moon Unit, Diva, Dweezil, and Ahmet Rodan?

4. What is the title of The Mothers Of Invention's first album?

5. Zappa's set of doo-wop parodies appears on what 1968 album?

6. Zappa and Ray Collins wrote what song for The Penguins?

7. When the Montreux Casino burned on the eve of a Mothers concert, what popular song described the event?

8. Frank Zappa and Captain Beefheart had planned to collaborate on a band and a film. Name both.

9. True or False: Modern classical composer Phillip Glass is Zappa's idol.

10. Zappa recorded a double-album sound track for a never-released film. Name it.

11. What two former Mothers formed the band Little Feat?

12. In which of these films does Zappa appear? **A.** *The World's Greatest Sinner;* **B.** *Baby Snakes;* **C.** *Run Home Slow;* **D.** *Valley Girl.*

13. What is the name of the film that Zappa co-wrote, co-directed, starred in, and scored?

14. What two British rockers co-starred in this 1971 film?

15. Which of these phrases was *not* popularized by the single "Valley Girl"? **A.** "Gag me with a spoon"; **B.** "Bag your face"; **C.** "Barf me out"; **D.** "Grodie to the max."

Frank Zappa (seated, wearing a sleeveless T-shirt) and The Mothers Of Invention. 57

ANSWERS

THE ALLMAN BROTHERS

(Page 2)

1. **(A)**, **(B)**, **(C)**, and **(D)**.
2. Fame Studios in Muscle Shoals, Alabama.
3. John D. Loudermilk.
4. **(C)** Stevie Wonder.
5. "Layla" (1970), with Derek And The Dominos.
6. New York's Fillmore East, in March of 1971.
7. They occurred within an area of three blocks.
8. Scooter Herring.
9. Great Southern.
10. *Two The Hard Way* (1977).
11. Gregg and Cher's son.
12. Chuck Leavell, Lamar Williams, and Jai Johnny Johanson.
13. Boz Scaggs. His album was called *Boz Scaggs*, also.
14. Two places: an advertisement for the band's home state, Georgia; and a line from T. S. Eliot's "The Love Song Of J. Alfred Prufrock."
15. "These Days," on *Laid Back* (1973).

THE ANIMALS

(Page 3)

1. Newcastle-on-Tyne, the British town in which the band was formed.
2. "House of The Rising Sun," in 1964.
3. The Farfisa organ.
4. "Monterey."
5. Eric Burdon.
6. Alan Price.
7. From a colorful army vet in their neighborhood named Animal Hog.
8. *Get Yourself a College Girl*.
9. **(A)**, **(D)**, **(B)**, **(C)**.
10. Chas Chandler.
11. Andy Summers, now of The Police.
12. Because of his fear of flying—he didn't want to tour outside the U.K.
13. *Comeback*.
14. *Before We Were So Rudely Interrupted*.

THE BAND

(Page 4)

1. Levon Helm of Marvell, Arkansas. The others were born in Canada.
2. John Hammond, Jr.
3. Robbie Robertson and Levon Helm.
4. The Band's house in Saugerties, New York.
5. Van Morrison.
6. *Moondog Matinee* (1973). Named after Alan Freed's radio show, the album consisted primarily of old rock 'n' roll songs.
7. *Beautiful Noise* (1976).
8. Levon Helm.
9. *The Basement Tapes*.
10. *The Last Waltz* (1978), directed by Martin Scorsese.
11. The RCO All-Stars.
12. *Coal Miner's Daughter* (1980). He played Loretta Lynn's father.
13. *Carny*.
14. On "Between Trains," a cut on the sound track from *The King of Comedy* (1983).

THE BEACH BOYS

(Page 5)

1. Just one—"Good Vibrations."
2. Judy Bowles, who was Brian Wilson's girlfriend.
3. Dennis Wilson.
4. **(B)** Murray Wilson, manager of the band and the father of Brian, Carl, and Dennis. Al Jardine was an original member of the band.
5. Brian Wilson.
6. 1975.
7. Maharishi International University (in Fairfield, Iowa), where the main course of study includes Transcendental Meditation.
8. Glen Campbell.
9. Brother. The other group was "Flame," from whose ranks guitarist Blondie Chaplin and drummer Ricky Fataar later joined The Beach Boys.
10. Six: Brother, Capitol, Caribou, Reprise, X, and Candix.
11. Charles Lloyd (1978).
12. *Stack O' Tracks* (1968).
13. "Don't Worry Baby."
14. Dennis Wilson; "Never Learn Not To Live."
15. True. The ballet was first performed on March 1, 1973.

THE BEATLES

(Page 6)

1. **(B)** "All My Loving."
2. "I Want To Hold Your Hand."
3. "My Bonnie" (1961). The Beatles (credited as The Beat Brothers) backed singer Tony Sheridan.
4. Tommy Moore. He was replaced by Best in August, 1960.
5. Stu Sutcliffe, who left the group in April, 1961, to become a painter. He played bass, poorly.
6. He managed his father's record store, NEMS Records. A customer's request for "My Bonnie" led him to The Beatles.
7. The Beatles auditioned for producer George Martin in June. In August, Ringo Starr replaced Pete Best.
8. 1—**(D)** John's son Julian; 2—**(A)** Paul's dog; 3—**(B)** John's mother; 4—**(C)** Maharishi Mahesh Yogi.
9. Incredibly, none of them were the top album of the year, an honor based not on sales but on weekly chart positions. In 1967, for example, *Sgt. Pepper's* was ranked #10. *More Of The Monkees* and *The Monkees* were ranked first and second, respectively.
10. "Yesterday." Paul wrote the music and couldn't think of any other words for a few days.
11. Candlestick Park in San Francisco, August 29, 1966. Their last public performance of any kind was held on the rooftop of Apple during the *Let It Be* sessions.
12. They all released albums on The Beatles' Apple label.
13. They recorded Lennon and McCartney songs that The Beatles never recorded.
14. Eric Clapton.
15. *Yesterday And Today* (1966), which contains tracks omitted from earlier American albums (but included on the British versions). The original cover featured lumps of meat and mutilated dolls; the albums were recalled and a new cover pasted on.
16. **(C)** Blue Jay Way is a real place, but it's in Los Angeles.
17. Via the swift vengeance of "Maxwell's Silver Hammer."
18. This traditional English song was the first non-Beatle composition to be included on an album since their earliest days.
19. John is the preacher (white suit); Ringo is the mourner (black suit); George is the grave digger (denim clothing); Paul, of course, was the barefoot "corpse."
20. William Campbell, a Scot, took over for Paul in 1966 after a terrible car accident took the real McCartney's life.
21. "Cranberry sauce."
22. As a tribute, Booker T. & The MGs covered *Abbey Road* on their *McLemore Avenue* (1970), named for the Memphis street where their studio was located. Even the sleeve photo was duplicated: The band was shown crossing the titular street.
23. "Yesterday."
24. "This Boy."
25. **(D)** Rory Storme And The Hurricanes, the name of Ringo's group before he joined The Beatles.

THE BEE GEES

(Page 8)

1. Robin and Maurice (born December 22, 1949). Barry was born September 1, 1947.
2. Brothers Gibb.
3. Brisbane, Australia.
4. Robert Stigwood, who went on to found RSO Records.
5. *Solid Gold*.
6. **(C)** "New York Mining Disaster 1941" (1967). **(A)** "Spicks And Specks" (1967) was their first British chart hit; **(B)** "Three Kisses of Love" (1963) was their very first single; **(D)** "How Can You Mend A Broken Heart" (1971) was their first No. 1 hit in America.
7. Dick Clark's *American Bandstand* in 1967.
8. Barry Gibb.
9. False. Sound tracks for *Mary Poppins* (1965) and *West Side Story* (1962–1963) also topped the year-end charts.
10. Until Michael Jackson's *Thriller* (1984).
11. Yvonne Elliman.
12. Three—"Stayin' Alive," "Night Fever," and "How Deep Is Your Love." Andy Gibb recorded "Love Is Thicker Than Water," and Samantha Sang recorded "Emotion."
13. **(B)** Neil Sedaka.
14. Lulu.
15. "How Deep Is Your Love."

CHUCK BERRY

(Page 9)

1. He worked on a GM assembly line, and studied hair dressing at night.
2. The Duck Walk.
3. "Maybellene" (1955).
4. "My Ding-a-Ling" (1972).
5. **(B)** *Rock Around The Clock*, which starred Bill Haley And The Comets.
6. "Bye Bye Johnny" and "Go Go Go."
7. A Cadillac Coupe de Ville.
8. The amusement park that Berry built in Wentzville, Missouri.
9. "Ida Red." Berry renamed it after a cow in a children's story he remembered.
10. *Let The Good Times Roll* (1973).
11. **(C)** Muddy Waters. Willie Dixon **(A)** played bass on most of Berry's early hits; Johnnie Johnson **(B)** played piano in Berry's first trio.
12. Transporting a minor across state lines for immoral purposes. He served a two-year sentence.
13. "Come On" (1963).
14. For stealing his style of guitar playing.
15. Income tax evasion.

DAVID BOWIE

(Page 10)

1. David Jones. He changed it to avoid confusion with Davy Jones of The Monkees.
2. Peter Frampton.
3. **(C)** clothing designer.
4. An astronaut that Bowie sings about in two of his most popular songs; he dies in an out-of-control space capsule.
5. "Fame"; John Lennon.
6. **(D)** all of the above.
7. **(C)** *Cat People*. He only sang the title song.
8. **(A)** and **(D)**. **(A)** Iggy Pop is a prototype punk rocker, and Zowie Bowie **(D)** is Bowie's 13-year-old son. Screamin' Lord Byron **(B)** is the drugged-out rock star in *Jazzin' For Blue Jean*; Ziggy Stardust **(C)** was a fictional rock legend Bowie portrayed on stage and record.
9. The left is gray, the right is blue. The pupil of the left eye was damaged in a childhood fight.
10. "Space Oddity" *(Man Of Words, Man Of Music)*; "Ashes To Ashes" *(Scary Monsters)*.
11. *ChangesOneBowie* (1976).
12. "Angie" (1973).
13. Ziggy Stardust's backup band (guitarist Mick Ronson, bassist Trevor Bolder, and drummer Michael Woodmansey).
14. True. Also in a touring company that crossed the country.
15. They are all names of bands that featured Bowie prior to his 1966 name change. Each released a single.

JAMES BROWN

(Page 11)

1. Picked cotton, committed armed robbery, and became a semi-pro boxer and baseball player, among other things.
2. Little Richard.
3. The gospel-influenced R&B band (originally known as The Swanees) that Brown became famous with in the late '50s.
4. "Please Please Please" (1956).

5. None. However, many of his hits did rise to the top of the R&B and Soul charts.
6. They're all correct.
7. Piano and drums.
8. Mick Jagger couldn't meet Brown's asking price.
9. Los Angeles mayor Sam Yorty.
10. Wayne Cochran.
11. They were the pseudonym used by Brown and his band, The J.B.'s, to record the hit "Mashed Potatoes" (1962). King Records then signed The J.B.'s to back Brown in the studio and as a separate act.
12. $4.5 million.
13. Brown performs in *The Blues Brothers* (A) and *Ski Party* (B). He scored *Black Caesar* (C) and *Slaughter's Big Rip-Off* (D).
14. Afrika Bambaata.
15. McDonald's.

THE BYRDS

(Page 12)
1. (A) The Beefeaters.
2. "Mr. Tambourine Man" in March of 1965. It was written by Bob Dylan.
3. "Eight Miles High" (1966).
4. Gram Parsons; country rock.
5. Clarence White.
6. Gram Parsons; The Flying Burrito Brothers.
7. The three were Chris Hillman, Michael Clarke, and Gene Clark.
8. Granny glasses.
9. Jim McGuinn.
10. Gram Parsons.
11. A Rickenbacker twelve-string.
12. Gene Clark and Chris Hillman.
13. Jacques Levy.
14. *McGuinn, Clark & Hillman.*
15. True. It was during the folk segment of Darin's set.

ERIC CLAPTON

(Page 13)
1. The Yardbirds, John Mayall's Bluesbreakers, Cream, Blind Faith, and Derek And The Dominos.
2. "Slowhand."
3. "Sunshine Of Your Love" (1968).
4. "While My Guitar Gently Weeps" (1968).
5. Jeff Beck preceded Clapton, while Jimmy Page followed him.
6. He was dissatisfied with the group's artistic direction. He thought *For Your Love* and *Heart Full Of Soul* were too commercial.
7. "Clapton Is God."
8. Patti Boyd Harrison, who was married to Clapton's friend, George Harrison, at the time of the song's writing. She became Mrs. Clapton in 1979.
9. Blind Faith.
10. "After Midnight," off *Eric Clapton* (1970).
11. "I Shot The Sheriff" (1974).
12. "Sign Language." The two sing it together on the album *No Reason To Cry* (1976).
13. He had to have his pants taken out to accommodate some recent weight gain.
14. *The Last Waltz.*
15. He was hospitalized in St. Paul, MN, with a perforated stomach ulcer.

THE CLASH

(Page 14)
1. The 101'ers.
2. He was known for playing "Johnny B. Goode" on his ukelele in various London subway stations.
3. Viewing The Sex Pistols.
4. London SS.
5. Tory Crimes.
6. Mick Jones noticed the term "clash" repeatedly in the newspapers.
7. Keith Levene.
8. They opened for The Sex Pistols in the summer of '76.
9. March, 1977.
10. They were accused of shooting prize pigeons.
11. February, 1979.
12. *Rude Boy.*
13. *Sandinista!* (1981).
14. Original drummer Tory Crimes rejoined.
15. "Rock The Casbah."

CROSBY, STILLS, NASH & YOUNG

(Page 15)
1. Buffalo Springfield.
2. Because of creative differences with Roger McGuinn, among them McGuinn's refusal to record Crosby's "Triad," a song about a ménage à trois.
3. The Hollies.
4. Crazy Horse. The album is titled *Everybody Knows This Is Nowhere* (1969).
5. Rick James.
6. Robert Kennedy.
7. Judy Collins.
8. Graham Nash and Joni Mitchell.
9. In May of 1970, four Kent State students were killed by National Guard troops.
10. "Woodstock" (1970).
11. In 1976, when he left the Long May You Run Tour because of a throat ailment.
12. *Harvest* (1972).
13. Eric Clapton and Jimi Hendrix.
14. Manassas.
15. "Just A Song Before I Go."

THE DOORS

(Page 16)
1. They both attended classes at the UCLA Graduate School of Film.
2. From a line by William Blake: "If the doors of perception were cleansed/All things would appear infinite."
3. (B) *The Lords And The New Creatures* and (C) *An American Prayer* (which was turned into an album in 1978). *A Feast of Friends* (A) was a film Morrison directed; *No One Here Gets Out Alive* (D) is the title of a 1980 biography about Morrison.
4. The Lizard King. He was first mentioned in *Waiting For The Sun* (1968); a complete rendition of "The Celebration Of The Lizard King" appears on *Absolutely Live* (1970).
5. The Human Be-In; San Francisco's Fillmore Auditorium.
6. True.

7. (B) *The Soft Parade* (1969), The Doors' fourth album. (C) *Other Voices* (1971) and (A) *Full Circle* (1972) were recorded after Morrison's death. (D) *The Golden Scarab* (1975) was a Ray Manzarek solo album.
8. He claimed his parents were dead; they weren't. His father was a rear admiral in the navy. Morrison also dropped one "s" from his family surname, Morrisson.
9. He hassled a stewardess.
10. For indecent exposure.
11. "Hello I Love You"; Ray Davies of The Kinks sued in behalf of his composition, "All Day And All Of The Night."
12. Butts Band (B) was formed by guitarist Robby Krieger and drummer John Densmore in 1975; Nite City (D) was a short-lived band put together by Ray Manzarek. *Bobby Krieger And Friends* (A) was a 1977 jazz album; X (C) was a Los Angeles-based group produced by Ray Manzarek.
13. "The End"; *Apocalypse Now.*
14. The Hard Rock Cafe.
15. He died in a bathtub in Paris, in July, 1971, of a reported heart attack. He's buried in the "Poet's Corner" of Paris' Père Lachaise cemetery.

BOB DYLAN

(Page 17)
1. Robert Allen Zimmerman. He changed it in the early '60s in honor of Dylan Thomas.
2. "Like A Rolling Stone"; "Rainy Day Women #12 & 35."
3. Harry Belafonte's *Midnight Special* (1960). Dylan was paid $50 for his harmonica playing.
4. Woody Guthrie, who was in a New Jersey hospital.
5. Joan Baez.
6. "You Gotta Serve Somebody" (Best Rock Vocal Performance, Male).
7. For playing "electric music" with The Paul Butterfield Blues Band.
8. "Talking John Birch Society Blues" and "Let Me Die In My Footsteps," removed by then-CBS attorney Clive Davis.
9. *Renaldo And Clara* (1978). Ronnie Hawkins plays Dylan; Dylan portrays Renaldo.
10. (C) William Burroughs.
11. *Pat Garrett And Billy The Kid* (1973).
12. Beat poet Allen Ginsberg.
13. Columnist and author Pete Hammill.
14. A near-fatal motorcycle accident; he was in critical condition for weeks.
15. The "Tribute To Woody Guthrie" concert at Carnegie Hall on January 20, 1968.

THE EVERLY BROTHERS

(Page 18)
1. On *Arthur Godfrey's Talent Scouts* program.
2. False. Don was born February 1, 1937; Phil was born January 19, 1939.
3. Felice and Boudleaux Bryant.
4. (A) "Wake Up Little Susie."
5. Calliope Records.

6. Join the Marines.
7. Bo Diddley, Little Richard, and The Rolling Stones.
8. "Cathy's Clown," which sold more than two million copies and stayed on the charts for 17 weeks.
9. The Everly Brothers broke up. At the concert, Phil smashed his guitar and stormed off stage. It was nearly a decade before the two were reunited on stage.
10. To write songs.
11. *Johnny Cash Presents The Everly Brothers Show* was broadcast on ABC-TV from July to September, 1970. It was the summer replacement for *The Johnny Cash Show.*
12. "When Will I Be Loved."
13. Cadence (1957–1960); Warner Bros. (1960–1972); RCA (1972–1973); Mercury (1983–).
14. Ike and Margaret Everly were country stars known throughout the Midwest and South.
15. Dave Edmunds and Paul McCartney.

FLEETWOOD MAC

(PAGE 19)
1. Drummer Mick Fleetwood and bassist John McVie, who founded the group back in 1967.
2. False. She and Lindsey Buckingham were "discovered" when the band checked out the studio where their album, *Buckingham Nicks* (1973), was being recorded.
3. Christine Perfect; she had her own group, The Christine Perfect Band, which released several albums.
4. They never had a chart-topping single.
5. (C) Ronnie Lane.
6. The University of Southern California Trojan Marching Band played on *Tusk* (1979). They were recorded live at Dodgers Stadium.
7. They were third on the bill behind Jethro Tull and Joe Cocker.
8. They each left for religious reasons.
9. Mick Fleetwood.
10. Mick Fleetwood played drums for all of those bands before founding Fleetwood Mac.
11. A group put together by two former band members Dave Walker and Bob Watson. They later changed their name to Stretch.
12. *Fleetwood Mac In Chicago* (1969).
13. Tom Petty And The Heartbreakers.
14. Stevie Nicks and Lindsey Buckingham joined at the same time, in 1975.
15. Across from Frederick's Of Hollywood.

MARVIN GAYE

(Page 20)
1. (C) Aretha Franklin.
2. The Marquees; their single was "Wyatt Earp."
3. The Moonglows.
4. Berry Gordy, Jr., founder of Motown.
5. Gaye was instructed by the court to record an album, *Here, My Dear* (1978), and give wife Anna $600,000 in royalties. She later threatened to sue for invasion of privacy.
6. He was the session drummer at Motown.

ANSWERS

7. *What's Going On* (1971).
8. He went out for running back for the Detroit Lions.
9. A suitcase full of one million dollars cash.
10. He was shot by his father, an Apostolic preacher.
11. "I Heard It Through The Grapevine"; *The Big Chill* (1973).
12. The full title is "Mercy Mercy Me (The Ecology)."
13. **(C)** *Trouble Man* (1972). *Shaft* (1971) was scored by Isaac Hayes; *Superfly* (1971) was scored by Curtis Mayfield; *Cool Breeze* (1972) was scored by Quincy Jones.
14. *Midnight Love* (1982); the single was "Sexual Healing."
15. "How Sweet It Is (To Be Loved By You)" (originally recorded by Gaye in 1965).

THE GRATEFUL DEAD

(Page 21)

1. The Warlocks.
2. From an entry in the Oxford English Dictionary about an Egyptian prayer.
3. **(B)** *Electric Kool-Aid Acid Test* was a Tom Wolfe book about Ken Kesey and the San Francisco acid scene.
4. The middle finger of the right hand.
5. Pedal steel guitar.
6. "Bummer."
7. Kingfish and Bobby And The Midnights.
8. False. The Dead were one of the first groups to carry their own custom-designed state-of-the-art sound system with them from concert to concert. Weighing 23 tons, it would take a crew of nine to set it up and tear it down.
9. Ron "Pigpen" McKernan was an original member of the band; he played keyboards and the harmonica. A heavy drinker, McKernan left the band in 1973 and died shortly thereafter of liver disease.
10. *Shakedown Street* (1978).
11. **(A)** New Riders Of The Purple Sage. Garcia did session work with Jefferson Airplane **(B)**; drummer Mickey Hart worked with The Diga Rhythm Band **(C)**; drummers Hart and Bill Kreutzmann formed a band called Rhythm Devils **(D)**.
12. None.
13. The extended tracks and experimental studio work left the band deeply in debt to their label, Warner Bros., for studio time.
14. The Allman Brothers and The Band.
15. Stanley backed the band financially at the start, and later supervised construction of their sound system.

JIMI HENDRIX

(Page 22)

1. The Monkees.
2. The Monterey Pop Festival, June, 1967.
3. Brian Jones.
4. **(C)** Tina Turner.
5. Fat Mattress.
6. Jimmy James And The Blue Flames.
7. Chas Chandler of The Animals.

8. *Electric Ladyland* (1968).
9. Eire Apparent, an Irish group.
10. He set his guitar on fire.
11. Bob Dylan's "All Along The Watchtower," which made it to number 20.
12. Timothy Leary.
13. George Frederick Handel.
14. "Hear My Train A-Comin'."
15. Devon Wilson, a girlfriend and confidante of Hendrix.
16. **(C)** The Ronettes.
17. "Memorial Song (Song For A Dreamer)."
18. John McLaughlin.
19. A picture of Jimi surrounded by naked women.
20. Billy Cox and Mitch Mitchell.
21. "Killing Floor," recorded live at Monterey.
22. The seven-headed cobra symbol, which appears on the cover of *Axis: Bold As Love*.
23. Three—*Are You Experienced?*, *Axis: Bold As Love*, and *Electric Ladyland*.
24. Gil Evans—*The Gil Evans Orchestra Plays The Music Of Jimi Hendrix*.
25. He played a Fender Stratocaster turned upside down—he was left-handed.

BUDDY HOLLY

(Page 24)

1. "That'll Be The Day" (1957).
2. Paul McCartney.
3. "Not Fade Away" (1964).
4. The wife of Cricket Jerry Allison.
5. True.
6. Their chartered plane went down in a field in Clear Lake, Iowa.
7. The chirp of a cricket. One was loose in the studio.
8. Waylon Jennings.
9. "It's So Easy," performed by Linda Ronstadt.
10. "Three Stars."
11. Eddie Cochran.
12. "American Pie," by Don McLean.
13. "It Doesn't Matter Any More."
14. 1—**(A)** "True Love Ways"; 2—**(C)** "Raining In My Heart"; 3—**(B)** "Well, All Right".
15. *The Buddy Holly Story*, starring Gary Busey.
16. Dion And The Belmonts, who went on to finish the tour.

THE JACKSONS

(Page 25)

1. Jackie is the oldest (born 5/4/51), followed by Tito (10/15/53), Jermaine (12/11/54), Marlon (3/12/57), and Michael (8/29/58).
2. Brother Randy, and sisters Janet, LaToya and Rebbie (Maureen).
3. False. Most of their early hits were written and produced by "The Corporation," a group of Motown staffers. The Jacksons didn't begin to have creative control until the late 1970s.
4. All of the above. Gladys Knight **(A)** first discovered the act, and Diana Ross **(B)** promoted them. Bobby Taylor **(C)** of The Vancouvers, a Motown group, arranged their audition for label executive Berry Gordy, Jr. **(D)**, who polished the diamonds-in-the-rough.

5. Michael's *Got To Be There* (1972); and Jackie's *Jackie Jackson* (1973).
6. Jehovah's Witnesses.
7. False. Only the first four—"I Want You Back," "ABC," "The Love You Save," and "I'll Be There." The next two, "Mama's Pearl," and "Never Can Say Goodbye" only climbed to No. 2.
8. Gary, Indiana; Encino, California.
9. His famous glove fell into a toilet bowl. It had to be rescued, washed, and dried.
10. He couldn't be shown holding or drinking Pepsi-Cola.
11. The snake is named "Muscles"; it's also the name of a Diana Ross hit written by Michael.
12. When The Jacksons left Motown (Jermaine stayed behind with his new father-in-law), the label retained the rights to the name.
13. Jermaine Jackson married Hazel Gordy, daughter of Motown chief Berry Gordy, Jr.
14. He was nominated for 12; he won eight.
15. For Katherine Hepburn (he'd promised her) and "the girls in the balcony."

JEFFERSON AIRPLANE

(Page 26)

1. Signe Anderson.
2. He taught guitar in Washington, D.C.
3. Zulu.
4. *Blows Against The Empire* (1970).
5. Shit.
6. The Matrix.
7. David Crosby.
8. **(B)** New Riders Of The Purple Sage.
9. Hot Shit.
10. "Somebody To Love," written by her brother-in-law Darby; and "White Rabbit," by Slick herself.
11. "Miracles," off *Red Octopus* (1975).
12. *Manhole*.
13. The daughter of Grace Slick and Paul Kantner.

14. "Hearts," off *Balin*.
15. Mickey Thomas.

ELTON JOHN

(Page 27)

1. Reginald Kenneth Dwight.
2. At radio station WPLJ in New York, becoming the first live LP taken from a radio concert.
3. Saxophonist Elton Dean and singer Long John Baldry.
4. "Your Song" (1971), off the album *Elton John*.
5. Hercules.
6. "Lucy In The Sky With Diamonds" (1974).
7. Madison Square Garden; Thanksgiving Day, 1974.
8. Both recorded for Elton's own Rocket Records.
9. A $25 million policy.
10. Percussionist Ray Cooper.
11. Yoko Ono and her son, Sean Ono Lennon.
12. Marilyn Monroe.
13. Steampacket.
14. Long John Baldry, who talked Elton out of getting married to a woman who expected Elton to give up his music.
15. "Don't Go Breaking My Heart" (1976).

JANIS JOPLIN

(Page 28)

1. Joplin. It was her nickname.
2. Big Brother And The Holding Company, The Janis Joplin Revue, and The Full-Tilt Boogie Band.
3. An image of a bracelet.
4. All three were managed by Albert Grossman.
5. "Me And Bobby McGee," released posthumously.
6. "Piece Of My Heart" (1968).
7. Jimi Hendrix' death.
8. "Buried Alive In The Blues" (1971).
9. Southern Comfort, straight from the bottle.

Michael Jackson in "Thriller."

Elton John

13. He couldn't stand wearing the makeup all the time.
14. He was made up to look like a fox.
15. False. The band was biggest in America and Japan.

LED ZEPPELIN

1. The Who's Keith Moon, who told Jimmy Page that the band would go over like a lead balloon.
2. Vanilla Fudge (1969).
3. P.J. Proby.
4. While both backed Donovan on his *Hurdy Gurdy Man* album (1968).
5. Drummer B.J. Wilson (of Procol Harum) and singer Terry Reid.
6. (B) 30 hours.
7. Terry Reid, who was originally approached as vocalist.
8. (B) "Whole Lotta Love" (#4, 1969).
9. It was never issued to the public as a single.
10. *The Song Remains The Same.*
11. Six. It won a Grammy for Best Album Package of the year.
12. The sleeve was "moveable," like a children's book, revealing different objects in windows of buildings.
13. The sound track to *Death Wish II* (1982).
14. *Pictures At Eleven* (1982) and *The Principle of Moments* (1983). Both were recorded for Zeppelin's Swan Song records.
15. The Honeydrippers; *The Honeydrippers, Volume One* (1984).

LITTLE RICHARD

(Page 32)
1. Penniman.
2. He was 19; they were recorded for RCA in 1951.
3. "Bumps" Blackwell.
4. They were recorded in New Orleans for Los Angeles-based Specialty Records.
5. "Tutti Frutti," "Long Tall Sally," "Reddy Teddy," and "Rip It Up."
6. Jimi Hendrix.
7. (B) *Rock Rock Rock.*
8. He threw $8,000 worth of personal jewelry into a river.
9. The Toronto Peace Festival (1970).
10. *Rockin' With The King.*
11. He co-wrote "Long Tall Sally."
12. The Upsetters.
13. Dee Clark.
14. Seventh Day Adventist.
15. False. He mounted several comeback attempts — including three R&B albums for Reprise in the early '70s — after failing to gain commercial appeal with his gospel recordings.

BOB MARLEY

(Page 33)
1. Haile Selassie, emperor of Ethiopia and known by Rastafarians as The Lion Of Judah.
2. They co-founded The Wailers under their stage names of Peter Tosh and Bunny Wailer.
3. (C) *Catch A Fire* (1972, Island). (A) "Judge Not" (1961) was Bob Marley's debut record; (B) "Simmer Down" (1964) was his first hit single in Jamaica; (D) "Exodus" was his first British hit single, and a 1977 album on Island Records.
4. "I Shot The Sheriff" (#1, 1974).
5. Tuff Gong.
6. He didn't want to tour, and was reportedly unhappy with a new record deal.
7. "Roots, Rock, Reggae" (#51, 1976).
8. He convinced political rivals Michael Manley and Premier Edward Seaga to shake hands.
9. Sly And The Family Stone.
10. Zimbabwe.
11. The Rolling Stones' Mick Jagger and Keith Richards.
12. True. He worked in a Chrysler plant for most of 1977 in Wilmington, Delaware, where his mother lived.
13. Soul singer Johnny Nash, with whom Marley signed on as a songwriter.
14. The I-Threes (wife Rita, Judy Mowatt, and Marcia Griffiths).
15. False; he survived the assassination attempt in 1976. He died in 1980 of cancer.

JONI MITCHELL

(Page 34)
1. The ukelele.
2. She was born in Alberta, Canada; her given name is Roberta Joan Anderson.
3. (C) an artist.
4. David Crosby.
5. Label executive David Geffen.
6. No. She was scheduled to appear, but didn't leave her hotel room because she was advised (incorrectly, it turned out) that she couldn't perform and make it back in time for a scheduled appearance on *The Dick Cavett Show.*
7. 1 — (D) Crosby, Stills, Nash & Young; 2 — (C) Judy Collins; 3 — (A) Tom Rush; 4 — (B) Fairport Convention.
8. Charles Mingus. The album was *Mingus* (1979).
9. Crosby, Stills, Nash & Young.
10. Neil Young.
11. *Shadows And Light* (1980).
12. False. It never even made it into the Top 20.
13. She married her bass player, Larry Klein, in 1982.
14. Joni Mitchell. Most of her albums feature her original artwork.
15. During her set a man jumped on stage, grabbed the mike, and shouted: "This is just a hippie concentration camp!"

PETER, PAUL & MARY

(Page 35)
1. Greenwich Village, N.Y.
2. He was a comedian.
3. May, 1962; Warner Bros. Records.

10. *The Rose* (1979), with Bette Midler.
11. "Mercedes Benz" (1971).
12. Guitarist Sam Andrews.
13. The Monterey Festival in August of 1967.
14. (B) *Big Brother And The Holding Company* (1967); (A) *Cheap Thrills* (1968); (D) *I Got Dem Ol' Kozmic Blues Again* (1969); (C) *Pearl* (1971).

THE KINKS

(Page 29)
1. (D) *Kinda Kinks* (1965); (B) *Everybody's In Showbiz* (1972); (A) *Sleepwalker* (1977); (C) *Give The People What They Want* (1981).
2. The Ravens.
3. *Arthur (Or The Decline And Fall Of The British Empire),* written for a British TV program that never aired.
4. "Death Of A Clown" (1967).
5. "Lola," off *Lola Versus Powerman And The Moneygoround* (1970).
6. He had to change "Coca-Cola" to "cherry cola."
7. Konk Records.
8. Van Halen.
9. The Pretenders.
10. *One For The Road.*
11. Chrissie Hynde Kerr.
12. It is named *AFLI-3063* (1980), after the bar code on the LP cover.
13. (A) *Percy* (1971); and (D) *Virgin Soldiers* (1969).
14. He was a Golden Gloves boxer and soccer player.

KISS

(Page 30)
1. Wicked Lester.
2. Through ads in *Rolling Stone* (Peter Criss) and *The Village Voice* (Ace Frehley).
3. Teaching public school at P.S. 95 in New York City.
4. Drummer Peter Criss had the cat-like makeup; Ace Frehley wore the large star over his eye.
5. (B) Eric Carr. He played drums after Peter Criss left the group.
6. The band members added drops of their blood to the red ink.
7. Seven inches.
8. Anthony Zerbe; the film is set at an amusement park.
9. (A) biting off the head of a bird. Heavy-metal legend Ozzy Osborne does that.
10. All four band members released solo albums at the same time. Backed by a huge advertising budget, all four went platinum.
11. *Lick It Up* (1983).
12. Lou Reed.

ANSWERS

Elvis Presley

4. "If I Had A Hammer."
5. Pete Seeger and Lee Hays of The Weavers.
6. Bob Dylan; "Blowin' In The Wind" and "Don't Think Twice, It's All Right."
7. It was thought to contain drug references.
8. John Denver.
9. 1967's "I Dig Rock & Roll Music."
10. It was simply the catalog number of the album on Warner Bros.
11. 1970.
12. *Peter, Paul And,* and *Mary.*
13. He pleaded guilty to taking immoral liberties with a 14-year-old girl.
14. He now performs Christian music.
15. "Torn Between Two Lovers."

PINK FLOYD
(Page 36)

1. (A) David Gilmour. He replaced Syd Barrett.
2. *Tapestry* (1971), by Carole King.
3. *Animals* (1977).
4. *Piper At The Gates Of Dawn* (1967).
5. Syd Barrett, the group's founder, to whom the entire album, *Wish You Were Here,* is dedicated.
6. The Classical Music Festival at Montreux, September, 1971.
7. Free concerts.
8. It is a combination of the names of two Georgia blues artists, Pink Anderson and Floyd Council.
9. *More* (1969), *The Body* (1970), *Zabriskie Point* (1970), and *Obscured By Clouds* (1972).
10. False. They were the first to use 360-degree quadrophonic sound in concert, though.
11. The government of the Republic of South Africa.
12. Robert Wyatt. The album: *Rock Bottom.*
13. "No More Lonely Nights."
14. *A Nice Pair* (1973). It included *The Piper At The Gates Of Dawn* (1967) and *A Saucer Full Of Secrets* (1968).

15. They changed "don't give me that goody-goody bullshit" to "...bull-blank."

THE POLICE
(Page 37)

1. (C) John Mayall's Bluesbreakers.
2. Stewart Copeland.
3. Curved Air.
4. "Roxanne" (1978).
5. Stewart Copeland's solo project alias.
6. Teaching.
7. 1—(B); 2—(A); 3—(D); 4—(C).
8. Stewart Copeland.
9. Henri Padovani.
10. Gordon Sumner.
11. I.R.S. (International Record Syndicate), and F.B.I. (Frontier Booking International).
12. "Every Breath You Take."
13. *I Advance Masked* (1982); *Bewitched* (1984).
14. *Rumblefish* (1983).
15. *Lolita,* by Vladimir Nabokov.

ELVIS PRESLEY
(Page 38)

1. Pat Boone.
2. "That's All Right" (1954).
3. Al Jolson.
4. Bill Black, Scotty Moore, and D.J. Fontana.
5. Elvis Presley, Jerry Lee Lewis, Johnny Cash, and Carl Perkins.
6. *The Steve Allen Show,* July 1, 1956.
7. "Blue Suede Shoes."
8. "Heartbreak Hotel" (1956).
9. He was a truck driver.
10. "Are You Lonesome Tonight?"
11. *For LP Fans Only* (1959).
12. "Bridge Over Troubled Water."
13. "Tomorrow Is A Long Time" (1966) and "Don't Think Twice, It's All Right" (1967).
14. "Steamroller Blues."
15. 1—(B); 2—(A); 3—(D); 4—(C).

16. *King Creole* (1958).
17. "Aloha From Hawaii."
18. Eddie Rabbitt.
19. Sun Records.
20. Otis Blackwell.
21. Willie Mae "Big Mama" Thornton.
22. They released eight Presley singles simultaneously, including "Love Me Tender."
23. "If I Can Dream."
24. Ral Donner.
25. "My Happiness," an Ink Spots number that he recorded as a gift to his mother.

PRINCE
(Page 40)

1. True. His full name is Prince Roger Nelson.
2. That Prince be allowed to produce his own album, thus becoming the youngest person (he was 19) to do so in Warner Bros. history.
3. He played all the instruments himself.
4. "I Feel For You." It first appeared on *Prince* (1979), his second album.
5. (C) Francis L. That was the name of Prince's father in the movie *Purple Rain.*
6. It was one of the first videos by blacks to be shown on MTV, along with Michael Jackson's *Billie Jean.*
7. Dance, Music, Sex, Romance.
8. Only two: drummer Bobby Z, and keyboard player Matt Fink (The Doctor).
9. The producer and writer on albums by The Time, Vanity 6, Apollonia 6, and other Prince-related artists. Though he denies it, it's assumed to be a pseudonym for Prince.
10. *Dreams.*
11. The First Avenue And Seventh Street Entry in Minneapolis, Minnesota.
12. They're the real names for Vanity and Apollonia, the original co-star of *Purple Rain* and her last-minute replacement, respectively.
13. Lake Minnetonka, located in suburban Minneapolis.
14. Pop, R&B, and Dance charts.
15. She was the percussionist with Lionel Richie's band (her father was a percussionist with Santana).

LOU REED
(Page 41)

1. The Primitives. They released several singles on Pickwick Records, where Lou Reed had worked as a staff songwriter.
2. False. Andy Warhol took the group under his wing.
3. Nico (after one album), John Cale (after two), Maureen Tucker (after three), Lou Reed (during the fourth), and Sterling Morrison (after the fourth).
4. Delmore Schwartz.
5. "Walk On The Wild Side."
6. *Transformer* (1972); it was produced by David Bowie and Mick Ronson.
7. Andy Warhol designed a peelable illustration of a banana.
8. He smashed a piano to pieces.
9. Bassist Sterling Morrison.
10. Before moving to England to pursue a solo

career, he worked for a time at his father's accounting office.
11. *Fusion.* In 1977, he won an award from the Coordinating Council of Literary Magazines for his poem, "The Slide."
12. He'd pretend to be actually shooting up on stage.
13. Andy Warhol's mid-'60s mixed-media show in New York's East Village, where The Velvet Underground was the house band.
14. They recalled the album (an experimental work featuring machine hums and other noises) from distribution. Reed left the label shortly afterwards.
15. (D) *One-Trick Pony* (1980). He played a record producer.

THE ROLLING STONES
(Page 42)

1. Bassist Dick Taylor, drummer Mick Avory, drummer Tony Chapman, and keyboardist Ian Stewart were all members of The Stones in the early days of the band.
2. They met at Dartford Maypole County Primary School in 1950.
3. 1—(C) Chuck Berry; 2—(A) John Lennon and Paul McCartney; 3—(B) Buddy Holly; 4—(D) Bobby Womack And The Valentinos.
4. "(I Can't Get No) Satisfaction" (1965) was the first No. 1 song in America; "It's All Over Now" (1964) was the first British No. 1 hit.
5. Nanker Phelge.
6. "Let's Spend The Night Together." Sullivan wanted the lyric changed to "Let's spend *some time* together."
7. From a Muddy Waters song, "Rollin' Stone" (1948).
8. "We Love You" (1967).
9. "You're So Vain" (1972).
10. There were no leaves on his stem.
11. *Gimme Shelter* (1971).
12. The infamous concert at Altamont, California, where a concertgoer was killed by some Hell's Angels just a few feet from the stage.
13. False. George Lucas, creator of the *Star Wars* saga, was the soon-to-be-famous cameraman.
14. Marianne Faithful, Jagger's then-girlfriend.
15. True. He had already quit and been replaced (by Mick Taylor) when he died in his swimming pool.
16. At an outdoor concert, Jagger read poetry and released thousands of butterflies.
17. Stevie Wonder.
18. A picture of a bathroom wall covered with scatological graffiti.
19. Lucille Ball, Brigitte Bardot, Liza Minnelli, Marilyn Monroe, and Raquel Welch.
20. (A) *Performance* and (D) *Ned Kelly.* Jagger was supposed to co-star in *Fitzcarraldo* (B), but left after several weeks of filming when the production was forced to shut down. (C) *One Plus One* is a Jean-Luc Godard film featuring The Stones rehearsing and recording "Sympathy For The Devil."
21. Andy Warhol; it first appeared on *Sticky Fingers* (1971).
22. Peter Tosh.

23. (C) *Goat's Head Soup.*
24. Compass Point Studios, Bahamas.
25. A group formed in 1979 by Stones' guitarists Keith Richards and Ron Wood, with drummer Ziggy Modeliste and bassist Stanley Clarke. They toured, but never released an album.

ROXY MUSIC
(Page 44)

1. Brian Peter George St. John De Baptiste de la Salle Eno.
2. Pete Sinfield, King Crimson's lyricist.
3. Keyboardist and violinist Eddie Jobson.
4. "Love Is The Drug" (#30, 1975); "Avalon" (#27, 1982).
5. A new cover featured a photo of the trees and bushes the women were standing among. Some stores carried the original cover under an opaque green shrink-wrap.
6. *Viva* (1976), a live album; and *Greatest Hits* (1977).
7. Bassist John Wetton and Eddie Jobson.
8. They all played bass with Roxy Music at one time. The band never had a full-time bassist.
9. Kevin Ayers, John Cale, and Nico.
10. Robert Fripp.
11. A white tuxedo (or occasionally a black mohair suit).
12. Jerry Hall, who recently gave birth to Mick Jagger's daughter.
13. 1 — (B) *Music For Films;* 2 — (C) *The Bride Stripped Bare;* 3 — (A) *Listen Now.*
14. Humphrey Bogart.
15. "Jealous Guy" (off *Flesh And Blood,* 1980) was a No. 1 hit in Britain for Roxy Music.

SIMON & GARFUNKEL
(Page 45)

1. Tom and Jerry recorded "Hey Schoolgirl" in 1957. It reached No. 54 on the charts.
2. They first sang together in their Forest Hills, New York, elementary school. They became

professionals while enrolled at Forest Hills High.
3. (C) Arty Garr. Art Garfunkel recorded under that name after the break-up of Tom And Jerry.
4. "Sounds Of Silence." The acoustic version appears on *Wednesday Morning 3 A.M.* (1966); the remixed version appears on *Sounds Of Silence* (1966).
5. *The Graduate* (1968).
6. "50 Ways To Leave Your Lover" (1976).
7. *Annie Hall* (1977).
8. *One-Trick Pony.*
9. (B) *This Is Spinal Tap.* Art Garfunkel was featured in the other three.
10. On September 19, 1981, Simon & Garfunkel gave a free concert to 500,000 people on The Great Lawn in Central Park, New York.
11. A rally in behalf of George McGovern's presidential bid, held at Madison Square Garden in New York.
12. False. "All I Know" (1973) reached No. 9.
13. *Bridge Over Troubled Water* (1970) sold about nine million copies. The title song was their largest-selling single ever.
14. "My Little Town" (1975).
15. "(What A) Wonderful World," a cover of a Sam Cooke oldie.

SLY AND THE FAMILY STONE
(Page 46)

1. Sylvester Stewart.
2. He was a DJ at KSOL in San Francisco.
3. "C'mon And Swim."
4. The Beau Brummels; "Laugh Laugh."
5. The Stoners.
6. Keyboards and guitar.
7. "I Ain't Got Nobody" for the tiny Loadstone label.
8. "Dance To The Music" (1968).
9. "Everyday People" (1969).
10. "Family Affair" (1971).
11. Madison Square Garden.
12. He was the group's guitarist.
13. Bassist Larry Graham; Graham Central Station.
14. George Clinton.

15. He didn't show up for the show, causing a riot.

THE SPECTOR SOUND
(Page 47)

1. "Be My Baby" (1962); "Baby, I Love You" (1963).
2. Cher.
3. *A Christmas Gift For You.* (1963).
4. (B) The Ronettes.
5. Philles.
6. Donte.
7. "Say Goodbye To Hollywood."
8. (D).
9. *Let It Be* (1970).
10. Ike and Tina Turner.
11. "To Know Him Is To Love Him," by The Teddy Bears.
12. "Play With Fire."
13. Wall Of Sound.
14. The Concert For Bangladesh.
15. *Easy Rider.* (1969).

BRUCE SPRINGSTEEN
(Page 48)

1. Chicago.
2. "Hungry Heart" (1980).
3. He told the guards he'd recently been on the covers of *Time* and *Newsweek.*
4. Jon Landau of Boston's *Real Paper,* May 9, 1974.
5. The Boss; The Big Man.
6. (A) Anne Murray.
7. "Because The Night" (1978).
8. He narrated.
9. Nils Lofgren.
10. Robin Williams on *Throbbing Python Of Love.*
11. Brian De Palma.
12. Neither Springsteen nor the band are pictured in the clip.
13. 1 — (D); 2 — (B); 3 — (C); 4 — (A).
14. "...the Wisconsin night."
15. "Pink Cadillac," "Cadillac Ranch," "Used Cars," and "Stolen Car."
16. "Because the record company just gave me a big advance."
17. Manfred Mann (1976).
18. Cherry tops.
19. *New York, New York* (1977).
20. John Steinbeck's *The Grapes Of Wrath.*
21. Gary "U.S." Bonds.
22. Little Stevie And The Disciples Of Soul.
23. Springsteen played acoustic guitar.
24. Candy.
25. Wendy.

ROD STEWART
(Page 50)

1. *Every Picture Tells A Story* (1971).
2. The Jeff Beck Group.
3. *An Old Raincoat Won't Ever Let You Down.*
4. They dropped the "Small" from the name.

5. Britt Ekland.
6. Guitarist Ron Wood, keyboardist Ian McLagan, bassist Ronnie Lane, drummer Kenney Jones, and Stewart.
7. He played pro soccer.
8. A Lamborghini.
9. He played harmonica.
10. Jimi Hendrix.
11. Cat Stevens.
12. "Do Ya Think I'm Sexy?"
13. Wear pantyhose.
14. "You're In My Heart." She dropped the suit and settled out of court.
15. 1 — (B); 2 — (D); 3 — (A); 4 — (C).

DONNA SUMMER
(Page 51)

1. "No More Tears (Enough Is Enough)" (1979).
2. She won a role in a Munich, Germany, production of *Hair* in 1967.
3. Giorgio Moroder and Peter Bellotte.
4. Munich.
5. "Love To Love You Baby" (1975).
6. "MacArthur Park" (1978).
7. Richard Harris.
8. Jimmy Webb.
9. *Thank God It's Friday* (1978).
10. "Last Dance."
11. "Bad Girls" and "Hot Stuff."
12. Bruce Sudano, the lead vocalist for Brooklyn Dreams.
13. Quincy Jones.
14. Bruce Springsteen.

THE SUPREMES
(Page 52)

1. (A).
2. Detroit's Brewster Projects.
3. Diana Ross, Florence Ballard, and Mary Wilson.
4. RCA.
5. Cindy Birdsong replaced Florence Ballard.
6. Patti LaBelle And The Bluebelles.
7. Jean Terrell.
8. Eddie Holland, Lamont Dozier, and Brian Holland; they were known professionally simply as Holland/Dozier/Holland.
9. *Mahogany* (1975), *Lady Sings The Blues* (1972), *The Wiz* (1978).
10. "Muscles" (1982).
11. Mary Wilson. She formed Mary Wilson And The Supremes.
12. "Someday We'll Be Together" (1969).
13. "I'm Going To Make You Love Me."
14. (D) (1975); (B) (1978); (A) (1981); (C) (1982).

TALKING HEADS
(Page 53)

1. At the Rhode Island School Of Design.
2. The Artistics/The Autistics.
3. The Ramones.
4. Lani, Loric, and Laura.
5. "Take Me To The River" (1978).
6. Brian Eno.

Simon & Garfunkel

ANSWERS

7. *Mesopotamia* (1983).
8. Robert Rauschenberg.
9. Drummer Chris Frantz and bassist Tina Weymouth.
10. Nona Hendryx.
11. *Stop Making Sense* (1984).
12. *Remain In Light* (1980).
13. Frantz and Weymouth; The Tom Tom Club.
14. *The Catherine Wheel* (1983).
15. "Once In A Lifetime"; Toni Basil.

THE WHO

(Page 54)

1. He was imitating a mod on pills. Stuttering is a sign of amphetamine abuse.
2. It was insulting to stutterers.
3. Generation X; "Your Generation."
4. "I Can See For Miles" (#9, 1967).
5. "I Can't Explain" (1965); Jimmy Page.
6. They were declared to be the world's loudest rock band. In London on May 31, 1976, sound levels were measured at 120 decibels, at a distance of 50 yards.
7. (B) and (A).
8. Meher Baba.
9. Townshend called for a volunteer from the audience, and 19-year-old Scott Halpin from Muscatine, Iowa, finished out the set.
10. *Who's Next* (1971).
11. 1—(D); 2—(C); 3—(A); 4—(B).
12. (B).
13. John Entwhistle's early alias in The Who.
14. R-O-C-K.
15. *Tommy* (1975); *Lisztomania* (1975); *The Kids Are Alright* (1979); and *McVicar* (1980).
16. Townshend, a six-footer, accidentally hit his guitar against a low ceiling and broke it. The fans went wild.
17. "I Can't Explain" (1965).
18. "Anyway, Anyhow, Anywhere" (1965).
19. Keith Richards.
20. Holiday Inn.
21. Australia. They kept their promise.
22. Entwhistle.
23. Kief Spoon.
24. "Monterey" (1968).
25. *Empty Glass;* "Let My Love Open The Door."

STEVIE WONDER

(Page 56)

1. Steveland Morris.
2. The Rolling Stones.
3. *Music Of My Mind* (1972).
4. *Talking Book* (1972).
5. Minnie Riperton; "Lovin' You."
6. Cornrows braids.
7. He lost his sense of smell.
8. "Blowin' In The Wind" (1966).
9. Jeff Beck.
10. "Fingertips, Part 2" (1963).
11. *Muscle Beach Party* and *Bikini Beach.*
12. *The Secret Life of Plants.*
13. 1—(B); 2—(A); 3—(D); 4—(C).
14. "I Just Called To Say I Love You."
15. "Ebony And Ivory."

FRANK ZAPPA

(Page 57)

1. He was a government scientist who also played the guitar.
2. A "bicycle concerto," which included plucking the spokes and blowing through the handlebars.
3. Zappa's four children.
4. *Freak Out* (1966).
5. *Cruisin' With Ruben And The Jets* (1968).
6. "Memories Of El Monte" (1963).
7. "Smoke On The Water" by Deep Purple. The heavy-metal band was set to open for Zappa And The Mothers.
8. The band was called Soots; the film was titled *Captain Beefheart Meets The Grunt People.* Neither panned out.
9. False. Zappa's idol is composer Edgard Varèse.
10. *Uncle Meat* (1969). It was the last album recorded by the original Mothers Of Invention.
11. Lowell George and Roy Estrada.
12. (B) *Baby Snakes* (1979), an eclectic mixture of concert footage, live action, and clay animation directed by and starring Zappa. Zappa scored the low-budget *The World's Greatest Sinner* (A) and *Run Home Slow* (C). Zappa had nothing to do with 1983's *Valley Girl* (D).
13. *200 Motels* (1971).
14. Ringo Starr and Keith Moon.
15. They *all* were introduced, among other elements of the vocabulary unique to the San Bernadino valley.

Frank Zappa